Bowhunting Tactics

THAT DELIVER TROPHIES

A Guide to Finding and Taking Monster Whitetail Bucks

Steve Bartylla

Skyhorse Publishing

"With a portion of the profits from this book going to the Bowhunting Preservation Alliance, I was handed the rare opportunity to truly give something back to the sport that has provided my life with a fullness that is surpassed by precious few things. Many talk about the need to help protect the sport and recruit younger members. I'm extremely thankful that I've been given the chance to actually help accomplish those tremendously worthy goals."

Steve Bartylla

We hope each time you see this book on your shelf, you'll imagine kids enjoying archery in your local schools, young bowhunters finding opportunities to hunt in their communities, and seasoned bowhunters still able to spend quality time in the woods. Thanks to your purchase of this book, the Bowhunting Preservation Alliance will change these hopes into realities. Growing archery and bowhunting and saving our bowhunting heritage is our mission and everyone associated with this book wants to not only help you be a better bowhunter but wants you to help us build a solid future for archery and bowhunting.

Jay McAninch
CEO/President, Archery Trade Association

Copyright © 2007, 2012, 2017 by Steve Bartylla

Foreword © 2017 by Dr. Todd A. Kuhn

Skyhorse Publishing books may be purchased in bulk at special discounts for sales promotion, corporate gifts, fund-raising, or educational purposes. Special editions can also be created to specifications. For details, contact the Special Sales Department, Skyhorse Publishing, 307 West 36th Street, 11th Floor, New York, NY 10018 or info@skyhorsepublishing.com.

Skyhorse® and Skyhorse Publishing® are registered trademarks of Skyhorse Publishing, Inc.®, a Delaware corporation.

Visit our website at www.skyhorsepublishing.com.

10 9 8 7 6 5 4 3 2 1

Library of Congress Cataloging-in-Publication Data

Bartylla, Steve, author.
Bowhunting tactics that deliver trophies / Steve Bartylla.
volume ; cm
ISBN 978-0-9769233-8-1 (hardcover : alk. paper)
1. White-tailed deer hunting -- Records -- North America. 2. Bowhunting -- United States. 3. Bowhunters -- United States. I. Title.
SK301.B355 2007
799.2'7652'021--dc22
2007930667

Cover design by Woods N' Water Press
Cover photo courtesy of Steve Bartylla.

Print ISBN: 978-1-5107-1903-3
Ebook ISBN: 978-1-5107-1908-8

Printed in the United States of America

Table of Contents

Table of Contents

Dedication

I would like to dedicate this book to my mother, Bonnie Bartylla. Simply put, she dedicated her life to ensuring that my brother Joe and I could achieve virtually anything our minds could dream up. Raising both of us on her own, she refused any form of government assistance. Instead, back in the days when being a divorced woman was looked down upon, she worked two and often three jobs to support us. Sure, we were still poor, but Joe and I never realized it. Mom made sure we didn't by consistently going without so that her children had everything they needed, and so much more.

Of course, there's far more to raising children than providing them with objects. That's where mom truly excelled. Despite working so many hours, she was somehow always there for us when we needed her. To this day, I know she would drop everything to help us, if the need ever occurred. Thankfully, she no longer has to bail us out of jams.

However, that's also in large part due to her work as a mother. When we were growing up, she constantly drilled into our heads that we could achieve anything. Before we even began junior high, she had made it so clear that we'd be going to college that we never questioned it. Though she never shied away from teaching us lessons and disciplining inappropriate behaviors, there was never a doubt in either of our minds that she loved and supported us. With that type of foundation, we were set up to be successful. Because of that, anything we achieve truly is a reflection of the sacrifices she made and her skills at being a single parent. I owe her my life in more ways than one. Thank you Mom, simply for being the person you are and making me into the person I am.

Foreword

The spindly six-point inched forward, nibbling his way to within sixteen steps of my loblolly pine. A warm, wet blanket of early season air draped over me as I watched him in the food plot below. My breathing became labored, my respiration as spastic as my knees, which now rattled uncontrollably together.

Subconsciously, I fought to steady my wobbly legs as a bead of sweat rolled off the tip of my nose. Yardages raced through my adrenalin-addled mind as I struggled to solve the rudimentary distance equation. Frantically, I settled on "twenty-something" as my brain surrendered to sensory overload. I centered my thirty-yard pin on him and freed the broadhead.

The arrow shaft went whistling over his back, skimming through the greenery—settling somewhere near the field's edge. The buck whirled, switching ends as he hooved out of sight, melting into the woody shadows. There I stood—shaking, dazed, and deerless. So went my first encounter with an antlered whitetail.

Bowhunting is thrilling. However, needless to say—it is hard. Bowhunters embark on a long, solitary trek, saddled with a steep learning curve. Along the way, we hope to master an inanimate object, the bow. We also endeavor to master a wild creature, the whitetail.

While the mechanical machine is conquerable, sadly, we'll never solve the mostly unpredictable whitetail. The best we can hope for is to gain an elementary insight into what makes whitetails tick and how to maximize your opportunities while visiting their mysterious world.

Bowhunting knowledge is gained in two ways: 1) trial-and-error; and 2) learning from those who have successfully completed the journey before you. In the most general of terms, becoming a great bowhunter (as with most sports) is a skill set acquired from years-and-years of practice.

The most successful bowhunters have gathered a large number of in-field experiences. Each of these are earned from countless hours spent aloft, huddled in a treestand, crouched inside a cramped ground blind or belly-crawling over unruly terrain on innumerable spot-and-stalks. And, of course, long hours spent on the range honing and refining their shooting skills.

Collectively, these experiences are amassed and organized, forming a composite from which we draw upon while hunting. It is these experiences which ultimately determine success or failure. The more experience from which to draw, the better the bowhunter.

The bowhunting journey is fraught with many pitfalls and missteps along its way. Any one of which can ruin a hunt in short order. Harvesting a quality animal means minimizing or eliminating the mistakes. This is done by wringing out shooting errors from the equation, while perfecting the shot sequence on the range. However, unless you spend hundreds, if not thousands, of hours in the field, hunting errors are hard to avoid. That is, unless you are taught by reading the experiences of more seasoned and successful master bowhunters.

I shot my first bow, a Fred Bear recurve, some fifty-plus years ago. Since then, I have traveled the world in pursuit of many species. In those years, during which I have been both successful and have failed so miserably, I questioned my resolve to continue bowhunting. As with many, I spent my early bowhunting years learning almost exclusively by trial-and-error.

Learning by failing is frustrating, as it robs the joy from the bowhunting experience. Additionally, mistakes are costly both emotionally and monetarily. With each failure comes the pain of not capitalizing on a precious opportunity—one which rarely presents itself again. Failure squeezes our hunting dollars, as hunting equipment, leases, travel, and days away from work aren't cheap.

Shrinking the learning curve should be any good bowhunter's goal. I have learned that seeking the counsel of those more experienced is the best way to up your game. Whether these are expert shots and great shooting coaches or those who are gifted hunters. Those who consistently harvest quality whitetails, no matter the season or conditions—they are whitetail sages of sorts. One such master bowhunter is Steve Bartylla.

In *Bowhunting Tactics That Deliver Trophies*, Bartylla shares his unique experience and insight from his thirty-five-plus years in the field outsmarting the largest and most elusive whitetails. Bartylla reveals his secrets for formulating a winning game plan. This insight ranges from the basics, like the most overlooked pitfalls of successfully executing the harvest shot, to the very complex, such as outsmarting other hunters to score consistently on highly pressured public hunting grounds.

Whether you're a novice stretching a bow string for the first time, or a journeyman bowhunter with walls cluttered with trophies, rest assured *Bowhunting Tactics That Deliver Trophies* will help guide you along your bowhunting journey.

Dr. Todd A. Kuhn
Summer 2017

Acknowledgments

I can still remember it clearly: Sitting on the edge of an alfalfa field when a doe and fawn emerged from a distant wood line. With my heart in my throat, I watched them for the last 30 minutes of light. Though they never came closer than 200 yards of my tree, it was a thrill of a lifetime. Just that quick, I was hooked on bowhunting.

Cutting my teeth on bowhunting Wisconsin whitetails in the late '70s was a challenge. Deer populations were low, the big woods were seemingly endless, and experienced bowhunters were almost nonexistent. Somehow, I managed to take an adult doe at the age of 12, but looking back on it, all the stars in the heavens must have aligned themselves perfectly for it to occur.

Though the land around my home held many fields, the area I hunted mostly consisted of big woods and little agriculture. Furthermore, baiting wasn't an option. When that setting was combined with low deer numbers, simply seeing a deer was an event.

Then, of course, there was the equipment. At 11 years old, I began using a 45-pound Shakespeare recurve. Three years later, I picked up a second part-time job. The only reason I did it was to be able to afford a used Allen compound bow. I can still remember feeling so cool, as I lobbed arrows at targets with my very own compound! Little did I realize, and no one could have convinced me, that I'd been so much better off with the recurve.

At the same time all of this was going on, I was already well on my way to becoming a successful trapper. From the age of 10, I'd taken it upon myself to learn the art of trapping furbearers. Having caught a grand total of one muskrat that first year, I managed to improve my catch and expand my lines each year after.

Thanks to some very understanding professors, my college days found me running a trap line that exceeded 200 miles. The first day of each winter quarter, I'd talk to the professors and explain that trapping paid my way through college. If I didn't do it, I couldn't afford to go to school. I'd explain that, after the second week of class, I'd be gone for the rest of the quarter. Then I'd ask them what I could do in those two weeks to make up for not attending the rest of their classes. With their understanding, I'd bust my butt for those two weeks and be free for the rest of trapping season.

When thinking of acknowledgments, it occurred to me that these events and circumstances were the most significant in my development as a bowhunter. Learning to hunt deer in the big woods, where few deer existed in those days, taught me to scout and read sign. Simply put, if you didn't learn how to effectively accomplish those feats, you not only didn't kill deer, you almost never even saw them.

Because of such limited equipment, you also had to get close. Today, I routinely practice out to 70 and 80 yards. Though I've never taken a shot that far, today's archery equipment has made me more accurate at 80 yards than I was back then at 30 yards. In those early days, I needed to get within 15 yards of a deer if I wanted a realistic chance of scoring. That forced me to learn how to remain undetected.

Next, there was trapping. Over the years, I've applied so many of the lessons trapping taught me to hunting deer. The first was the need to know all you can about your prey. In trapping, the more I understood about fox biology and what made them tick, the more fox I caught. I found that knowing what furbearers wanted and how they acquired it was a major key to catching them. Applying that to whitetails only seemed logical.

Trapping also taught me to be creative. It was rare that I'd pull up to a bridge and find it ideal for a blind set that'd consistently produce mink. However, a little reconstruction would almost always produce the sets I needed. When trapping fence crossings, making one better and blocking the rest proved to be very productive. If a beaver run was a little too wide, making it smaller did the trick. Trapping taught me to make things work, as well as not to settle for a less-than-ideal setup. I can't tell you how many times I've done little things to improve a deer stand. That creativity came natural because of what I learned from trapping.

Finally, trapping taught me the importance of odor control. A sly fox could care less if the alarming odor he detects is coming from the trap, its stake, or some object the trapper touched. All it knows is that something is up and he's having no part of it. That trait forced me to think of every item he could detect, including myself, and learn to effectively treat it. When I finally realized that my odors were sabotaging my hunting efforts, it was only logical to approach dealing with a whitetail's nose in the same comprehensive manner. The advantage that has given me can't be overstated.

Because of all that, I would like to express my appreciation for northern Wisconsin, the few deer it possessed in my early years, the limited equipment available back then, trapping, and the professors who went the extra mile for me. Frankly, if it weren't for all of that, I don't believe that I'd be as qualified to write this book.

As far as professional acknowledgments are concerned, there are many. Anyone who has read that section in my previous book, *Advanced Stand-Hunting Strategies,* realizes that many magazine editors, cameramen and other industry professionals have been invaluable in helping me hone my skills. In no small part because of their help, I was able to become a full-time outdoor writer.

I must once again thank my friend Pat Durkin. He was the one who approached me and asked if I would be interested in doing a book for the Archery Trade Association. ATA president Jay McAninch made the financial commitment to make this book possible. Kate and Peter Fiduccia provided invaluable insight into what this book should cover, as well as the work involved with publishing it. If it weren't for those four individuals, this book would not have been possible.

I must also thank the readers of this book and all those who have followed my previous work. Before I began this profession, I can still vividly remember reading materials that I felt were written either to plug a product or enhance an ego, or were just plain baloney. Each time I felt personally insulted that I'd wasted my hard-earned money on it. When I began this career, I vowed to never forget that my true responsibilities lie with the audience of my work.

For that reason, I've made several vows that I refuse to break. Though I don't pretend to know all the answers and am not arrogant enough to believe I can never be wrong, I do promise that I sincerely believe every word I write.

Along those lines, because I used to base purchases on writers I respected, I have always refused to promote or endorse products that I wouldn't use if I had to buy them for myself. Out of respect to the reader, I am extremely careful when selecting products I endorse. To be honest, that approach has cost me considerable money over the years. However, I believe it easily pays for itself in both reader loyalty and my own self-respect.

The loyalty also goes back to the reader. I fully appreciate what it's like to be on your side of the aisle. One of the reasons that I still spend a portion of each season hunting heavily pressured public grounds is that I understand most of you have to compete with other hunters. I wouldn't feel qualified to try to teach others how to hone their hunting skills if I no longer hunted grounds similar to theirs. I can honestly say that I've never taken a buck out of a stand that I didn't scout and prepare myself.

Though I work extremely hard at what I do, I also understand that I'm extremely lucky to follow this profession. If it weren't for you, I would still be working a day job. Ultimately, you are my boss and the ones who sign my checks. For that, I sincerely thank you and acknowledge the impact that you've made on my increased ability to keep striving to become a better bowhunter.

Introduction

What are the keys to consistently taking trophy bucks? As I created the outline for this book, that is the question I spent countless hours pondering. On the surface, the answer involves being able to consistently place one's self within bow range of mature bucks.

However, that really is merely scratching the surface. First, one must find a location where accomplishing that feat is a realistic possibility. Then, the property must be analyzed to locate promising stand sites. Next comes getting stands in place. Unfortunately, this step is often complicated by the lack of suitable trees for stands. So one may be forced to get creative to make locations work, or choose to hunt from the ground.

Pulling off a successful shot is really the culmination of many details being successfully addressed.

Of course, if the scouting and stand prep is done during season, these activities must also be pulled off without alerting deer to our activities. Since most stand sites aren't good producers throughout the entire season, the hunter needs to determine which phase of the season the stand is ideally suited for. To not do so often results in wasted time and stands that burn out before they have a chance to heat up. Furthermore, hunters must also select routes to and from their stands that don't spook deer.

Obviously, none of that does any good if the hunters aren't in stand when the bucks stroll by. To maximize odds of that occurring, they must understand that certain stands produce best during specific times of day and under certain weather conditions.

Speaking of weather conditions, the hunter must also be prepared to master the elements. For most, the season goes fast and hunting opportunities are limited. The more weather is allowed keep hunters out of the woods, the fewer opportunities they are presented with. Knowing how to effectively dress for a wide range of conditions, and being equipped to endure them in relative comfort, is far too often an under-rated factor in success.

Even specific hunting tactics are overflowing with details. Should hunters call blindly? If so, do they go all out or take a subtle approach? How about using scents? What, where, how and why are all-important questions to answer when analyzing scent usage, and the answers hinge on a myriad of details regarding the habitat, how hard it's hunted, phase of season, and many other factors.

Ultimately, all of this is secondary if one doesn't capitalize on shot opportunities. There are seemingly countless ways for a hunt to blow up during this critical portion of it. The buck may see, hear or smell the hunter before the shot is presented. A flaw in form or poorly placed branch can send the arrow careening off course. Heck, a bad case of buck fever can shake some hunters so severely that they can't even attempt the shot. None of that even factors in equipment problems, rushing a shot, waiting too long or having the deer refusing to offer an ethical shot opportunity. A person could do an entire book simply on everything that can go wrong at the moment of truth.

Even after a shot, there are still the details of a successful tracking job to consider. Paying close attention to the shot and the events immediately following can make the difference between a celebration and depression. Pushing a deer too soon or not soon enough can both yield a bad result. One must also know what should be done when the blood trail is lost.

The longer I pondered the keys to taking trophy bucks, the clearer the answer became. Ultimately, bowhunting tactics that deliver trophy bucks rely on identifying and successfully addressing the details that are within the

Minnesota hunter Pat Reeve's astounding success is due to many factors. However, his attention to details is most definitely one of the most important.

hunter's control. After all, the act of consistently placing tags on trophy bucks is either due to possessing unbelievable hunting lands or the culmination of numerous details being attended to. Since I don't have access to that kind of property, and I'm guessing that most of you don't either, I chose to make this book very detail oriented.

The vast majority of the extremely successful hunters I know are fanatical about addressing the details. They realize that there are many things they can't control, so they obsess over dealing with the ones they can. The more details they successfully address, the fewer that are left to chance.

Minnesota hunter, and friend, Jim Hill once told me, "In life, with certain things, I can be fairly careless. When it comes to hunting, I don't leave anything to chance. If I can control it and do it, I will." One look at the bucks he's taken over the years clearly shows the value of such an approach.

Pat Reeve is yet another Minnesota hunter and good friend. Having hosted several shows, as well as producing a show of his own, Pat travels all over North America chasing trophy bucks. In one three-year stretch alone, these chases resulted in his taking of 26 Pope & Young class bucks, including three that grossed over the Boone & Crockett minimums. Having teamed with him on several stand-hanging missions, as well as having seen numerous other stand sites he's prepared, I can tell you that he is extremely picky. As his success illustrates, he knows what he needs for filming and killing trophy bucks and refuses to settle for marginal setups.

I also take an extremely meticulous approach to many aspects of hunting. At first glance, most of my cameramen think the odor-reduction techniques I force them to follow are over the top. They change their minds when bucks routinely appear unalarmed downwind.

I've been known to over analyze a property to death. When prepping stand sites in the spring, I can spend an hour in a 50-square-yard area trying to find the perfect tree, only to meticulously trim every single branch in shooting lanes covering the four sides of the eventual stand site. Sure, all the buck sign may be to the right side of the stand, but if one tries to slip by to the left, my three-foot-wide shooting lane won't have a single arrow-deflecting object impeding the shot. It's amazing how much smarter I've looked since I began creating shooting lanes in all four directions.

I could continue, but I suspect I've made the point. Consistently successful hunters fully realize how many things can go awry. They also realize that there are many potentially hunt-fouling factors they can't control—including the weather, other hunters, or a hot doe running in the opposite direction. To make up for it, the best hunters strive to meticulously address every detail they can. Simply put, they'll do all they reasonably can to be sure that they aren't responsible for blowing the deal.

The more I thought about it, the clearer it became what this book needed to focus on. What you will find in here is an honest and highly detailed approach to hunting.

If you're looking for a silver bullet, a magic potion or a shortcut to taking great bucks, you won't find it. Sure, I suspect that many of the details covered will automatically click and their importance will be instantly evident. On the other hand, many will likely seem trivial. However, try to remember that when enough little things are added together, they can deliver big results. With that in mind, let's begin covering the bowhunting tactics that deliver trophies.

Addressing little details, such as deciding to trim that one extra branch, can make the difference between a successful shot and a near miss.

1. Dress to Kill

The day was perfect. The temps were in the low 30s, with a steady west wind blowing at around 12 mph. Just before dawn, the mist began. Eventually building to a light rain, precipitation became my daylong companion. With bucks now regularly cruising for hot does, all the ingredients for a great day on the stand were there.

I was not to be disappointed. Over the course of my sit, my hunting logs show that I had brushes with nine different bucks, all but one falling in the 1.5- to 2.5-year-old range. It was the old timer that really got my heart pumping.

Around 12:30 p.m., I sensed something in the thicket behind me. Slowly turning my head, I caught a glimpse of the huge 12-point slipping through the tangle of cover. Seeing that his course would keep him out of bow range, I repositioned myself in the stand and exhaled a loud "ffffffffffffut, fffffffffffffut, fffffooooooooo" of a snort wheeze.

Immediately coming to a stop, the buck that would easily qualify for Boone & Crocket went into attack mode. He was undoubtedly the dominant buck in the area, and he was in no mood to be challenged, even by the phony snort wheeze I'd just created without the use of a call.

Hair raised on his neck, ears laid back into battle mode, the monster began stiff legging his way toward my stand. With my release already secured to my string loop, I could feel my body tensing for the impending shot.

At about the 40-yard mark, he was still making his way purposefully to my stand, and I believed that all I now needed was for him to turn and provide a good shot angle. With that, the monster would be as good as on my wall.

That's when everything fell apart. Hearing a crashing through the brush, both my head and the huge buck's snapped toward the sound. There, about 100 yards out, we spotted a little eight-point chasing an old doe. I knew right then that the huge 12's priorities had switched. Turning my head back to him, I was just in time to catch him standing still and watching the chase.

Knowing that it was now or never, I came to full draw. Still head on, I began praying in hyper speed that he'd turn for just a second before exploding after the pair that were so set on ruining this perfect encounter. In a single explosion of flight, the magnificent buck whirled and tore after the buck and doe. All I could do was let down my draw and hope that the mad chase would eventually lead the trio back to my stand.

Less than a half hour later, that wish was granted. Even in the wet conditions, the series of popping branches betrayed the approach of the chase. Then came the grunts. One after another echoed in the distance. I can only imagine the perplexed look I must have had. It sounded like a herd of bucks were storming the woods!

Bow in hand, I strained to see through the brush. A streak of white here, a blur of brown there, it seemed like the entire area was in motion. Then she came into view, pursued closely by seven different bucks! The young eight and huge 12 had been joined by a parade of others.

As the doe broke toward my stand, it appeared that I was catching the break I needed. Tragically, a pesky fork horn had a better angle and cut her off, veering her away from my position. As I came once again to full draw, the exhausted doe made it to within 25 yards of my tree before the troublesome fork steered her in the opposite direction. Many of the bucks entered shooting range. It was likely that a shout would have stopped more than one long enough for the shot. Unfortunately, the huge 12, as well as the original eight, weren't as fresh as the newer recruits and lagged just far enough behind to remain outside of bow range.

Over the next hour, two more bucks meandered through the area, following the scent of the doe on the cusp of estrus. Since neither broke into the 3.5-year-old class, I simply observed them as they slipped past my stand. With the chase having drawn the interest of every buck in the area, driving other does and fawns away, the remaining hours of the day passed without so much as a flicker of deer movement.

Returning to camp that night, the day's stories were exchanged. Though deer sightings ranged from a few to none, the one constant amongst the other hunters was that they had each suffered from the bone-chilling rain and wind enough to be driven from their stands well before noon. One unfortunate fellow had let it get to him so badly that by 8 a.m. he had been contemplating calling it quits. As he fidgeted in his stand, he was startled by the crashing departure of a shooter buck that had slipped to within 10 yards of his tree. I, on the other hand, had remained comfortable and focused the entire day.

THE IMPORTANCE OF STAYING IN THE GAME

I decided to begin this chapter with the long story of that rainy day because it illustrates so well the importance of comfort on the stand. As mentioned in the introduction to this book, staying in the stand is important— so much so that I firmly believe remaining comfortable is one of the most underrated factors in success.

Male testosterone levels are among the biggest culprits. For some odd reason, many hunters seem to believe it's macho to suffer on the stand. As I layered him up for a late-season hunt, my own son Zach once told me that

Not maintaining physical comfort can drive hunters from their stands early. At the very least, it draws their attention away from the true reason they are in the woods.

I was being ridiculous. Hunting is supposed to be about suffering and that, by making him wear all that cold-weather clothing, I was trying to turn him into a sissy. Upon hearing that, I smiled to myself and told him to only bring what he wanted. Less than an hour later, as he sat shivering in the stand next to me, he admitted that he wished he'd taken the "sissy" route. Shortly after that, when he found that he was too cold to draw back on the doe we'd come out to hunt, we returned to the truck.

Another reason that comfort is underrated is that many seem to have very short-term memory regarding how miserable hunting can be when comfort levels are severely compromised. We talk about how nasty it was and brag about braving the elements, but many of us often minimize the true suffering in our own minds. Sure, it was cold, but I toughed it out and it wasn't so bad. We somehow seem to forget that we couldn't stay still, were counting the minutes until we could leave, and ended up climbing down early.

Then there are also those who know better, but fail to plan ahead. Frankly, because comfort isn't as glamorous as a new deer call, a hot buck lure or the idea of hunting a fresh stand site, many overlook adequately preparing for being comfortable until they get bit.

Finally, some simply don't know the best methods of achieving comfort under various conditions.

Though this chapter is focusing on clothing, it's important to note that the comfort of the stand, whether it's on the ground or in a tree, is also an important consideration. True comfort is relative to each individual. In my case, I hate tree stands that don't offer a large platform and a soft, quiet seat. For all-day sits, having arm rests and a foot rest makes a big difference.

Regardless of why a hunter isn't comfortable, the cost is often steep. First, stating the obvious, if the hunter is too hot or too cold, at the very least, it drains much of the pleasure out of the hunt. Since almost all of us are doing this because it's fun, being uncomfortable defeats that purpose. Furthermore, being hot leads to increased odors, and being cold can not only make a shot more difficult, but also be life threatening.

Discomfort also distracts us from the other primary reason we're in the woods. Hunting is far more of a mental game than most give it credit for. When the hunter's head is in the game, he is far more alert, fidgets less and spends more time on the stand. The importance of those three things can't be overstated. Those who believe they have anywhere near as good a chance of taking a buck when they're miserable are only fooling themselves.

Let me repeat the point I just made. Keeping your head in the game and limiting movement, all while spending increased time in the stand, significantly increases the odds of killing a buck. Though a chapter on comfort

The author finds the Heater Body Suit to be unmatched for beating the cold, as well as providing him with the ability to regulate body heat so that he can remain comfortable in temps ranging from the high 30s all the way down into negative numbers.

isn't very glamorous, it very well may be the most important one in this book. Over the years, adequately addressing personal comfort will deliver more trophy bucks. That's a bold statement, but also a true one. And personal comfort is one of the few details that hunters have complete control over.

BEATING THE COLD

Before I begin this section, I feel the need to point something out: Over the course of this book, I won't be providing the specific names of many archery manufacturers or their products. The last thing I'll allow is for this book to become an infomercial. Those of you who are truly interested in what I use can figure most of it out from the numerous pictures of me in hunting situations.

However, there are times when product mentions can't be helped. In most cases, I'll only mention them when the product is unique, its use differs significantly from other products within its category or, in my opinion, it stands so far above any of the competitors that using anything else is a mistake.

The Heater Body Suit matches every one of those qualifiers. In the simplest terms, it's essentially a hunting bag with legs. Because of its superior insulation and ability to contain the body's own heat, it provides ultimate comfort from temps in the high 30s on down into negative numbers. I have used it when the thermometer read 15 below and the wind speed was above 20 mph. With the Heater Body Suit, I can honestly say that I was as comfortable as if I were sitting on the couch at home.

The Heater Body Suit is a highly effective shell that not only beats the cold, but also provides me with several other advantages. First, it allows me to dress light when traveling to the stand and know that comfort waits inside the suit. That eliminates the need to decide between working up a sweat as I walk or creating an odor plume by changing near my stand.

Dressing light also removes the chance of bulky clothing altering shooting form. This very real problem is eliminated because the suit slides from the hunter's shoulders when the bow is drawn. With a crisscrossing strap system holding it in place, the suit doesn't fall or create extra movement.

Additionally, being enclosed in the suit hides hand movements. Though it may seem trivial, the motion of simply drawing a grunt tube to my mouth or rattling antlers has resulted in previously unseen deer busting me cold. Since this movement is conducted almost exclusively inside the suit, that concern is nearly eliminated.

Finally, the Heater Body Suit's design gives a hunter the ability to remain comfortable in temperature changes ranging between double-digit negatives and 40 degrees. When the temps are in the 30s, I simply leave the zipper down and drape the suit over my shoulders. As the temp drops in the late afternoon, the zipper comes farther up until I'm comfortable again. This flexibility of function eliminates the need to bring extra clothing, as well as the extra movement and odors associated with putting on and shedding layers in stand.

The other option for beating the cold is taking the layered approach. When going this route, everything begins with the outer layer. To be most effective, it must possess several traits. Firstly, whatever you wear must have the ability to keep you warm. Comparing insulation ratings helps ensure that you select a suitable garment.

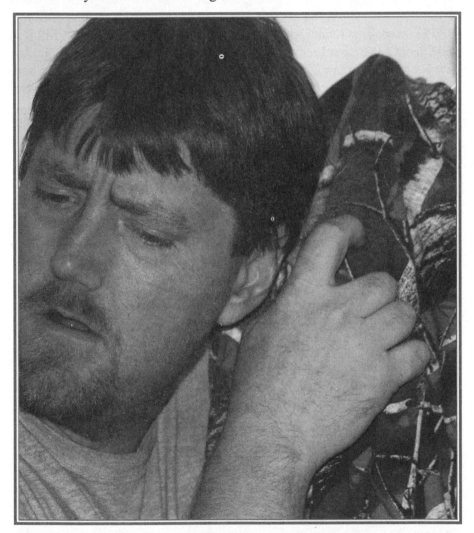

Giving hunting garments the scratch test before purchasing them will help you determine if they will be sufficiently quiet for use in the deer woods.

Remember to cater the clothing to the tactic. We all know this, but seem to forget at least once a year that it requires more clothing to stay warm while sitting on stand. However, the same clothing that isn't quite enough to keep us warm on stand will often cause us to overheat when stalking.

Secondly, it's critical that the outer layer be quiet. Sound seems to travel much farther and deer seem more sensitive to unnatural noises during late season. When considering an outer-layer purchase, try it on first and go through the motions involved with drawing a bow. Next, rub up against objects and scratch the fabric with your fingernails. Taking those easy steps will allow you to judge if the noise level it generates is acceptable or not.

Thirdly, the less bulk the better. Not only is walking in bulky clothing cumbersome, but that same bulk catches on vegetation and has a tendency to cause string slap. Neither typically leads to good outcomes while hunting.

Finally, it's not critical, but it's definitely nice when the outer layer is water resistant. Snow has a tendency to melt when contacting an outer layer. This in turn leads to the hunter getting wet and cold. If the garment is waterproof, that concern is completely removed. However, I've yet to use a waterproof garment that was as quiet as necessary for late-season hunting. Typically, water-resistant outer layers are the best balance between staying dry and allowing quiet movement.

After selecting a good outer layer, one must address the base layer. Here, warmth, comfort and the fabric's moisture-wicking properties are the biggest concerns. The reasons for choosing clothes that are warm and comfortable are self-explanatory. But moisture wicking is important as well because, even when one tries to avoid sweating, it will occur at times. A fabric that wicks the moisture away will keep you much warmer and more comfortable.

Fabrics and technology that kill, absorb or stop odors from forming are good choices. Because the base layer is the first line of defense against odors, it's always best to stop as many at that point as possible. Just remember that there isn't an odor-killing product available that will be effective when the hunter himself doesn't take all aspects of odor control seriously.

As for the middle layers, I have found fleece and wool clothing to be good choices because they both contain a surplus of air pockets for retaining heat. In windy conditions, I'll also use an inexpensive windbreaker as a middle layer. It constantly amazes me how much bulk can be shed by simply wearing a windbreaker directly under the outer layer.

Moving on to the feet, sock selection comes first. I've found a two-tiered approach best: A thin, moisture-wicking, odor-controlling sock should come first. Next, it's still hard to beat thick, wool socks for the outer layer. For what it's worth, I've never found a battery-operated sock to hold up to hunting activities for very long. As far as they're concerned, I keep my money in my wallet.

The choice of footwear is determined largely by whether one will be using a Heater Body Suit, a form of boot blanket or relying strictly on the boots to keep your feet warm, as well as whether you will be stand hunting or stalking.

If you're going to be stand hunting and relying strictly on boots for warmth, the lower their temperature rating the better. When deciding on a temperature rating, remember that they indicate the lowest temps that one can wear these boots while walking. There's a tremendous difference when one is sitting motionless.

Personally, I've always preferred wearing lightweight, rubber boots. This allows me to stalk or get to my stand quieter than I can in larger, warmer boots. It also reduces the amount my feet sweat when I'm walking. Before I began using a Heater Body Suit, I used chemical warming packs in my boots and slipped Boot Blankets over the tops. This combination, along with good socks, kept my feet warm.

Several other accessories designed for beating the cold can be tremendously helpful. Just as Boot Blankets and warming packs can allow a hunter to go light with boots, hand muffs and a chemical pack allow you to wear light-weight gloves or none at all. For people like me who hate shooting with thick gloves, the combination offers a very good solution.

Though not often thought of until after a bout or two with the cold, neck warmers serve a very useful purpose. Also, moving up to the mouth, it's hard to beat an Exchanger Mask for dealing with the brutal cold. Its unique design provides a steady stream of warm, moist air to the user's lungs, creating an amazing warming effect. Finally, a good, high-quality hat is worth its weight in gold.

With that, we are now set to battle the most frigid temperatures in comfort.

One word of caution: If you choose to take the layered approach, you have to practice shooting in the layers. We'll cover this in more detail later, but this is important enough to mention more than once. Simply put, bulk affects form, and changes in form alter arrow flight. The time to adjust pins for this is before the shot is taken at a buck of a lifetime. Afterward, it's too late.

BEATING THE HEAT

When trying to beat the heat, controlling excess odor is every bit as important to me as comfort. Being an odor-control fanatic, I do everything I can to ensure that my scent doesn't give me away. Sweat is an enemy to be battled at all times.

My approach begins by dressing as lightly as I can. For me, that means putting on underwear, socks and the lightest weight, most breathable carbon suit made.

Next, I pack in the very bare essentials. Though I always lean toward packing light, when it's hot I bring nothing but a rattle bag, grunt tube, my bow gear, some water, a small bottle of scent-killing spray and a zip-lock baggie of treated paper towels. Every ounce I can shed lessens the odds of sweating.

On the walk in, slow is the operative word. When battling terrain, I allow extra time for water breaks. Speaking of water, I freeze my water bottles and remove them early enough to allow partial thawing. Drinking ice water helps cool the body and prevent sweating.

Once I'm in the stand, I drink some more water and then towel down sweating areas with paper towels. These towels were sprayed with scent killing spray, allowed to dry and then stored in the baggies for just this purpose. Lastly, I spray myself with scent-killing spray. If it's so hot that I continue to bake while in stand, I carefully repeat the process every half hour.

When practical, stand selection can aid in beating the heat. Obviously, stands that allow the hunter to remain shaded will make staying cool much easier. Another helpful tool are the stand umbrellas that can be attached to trees. Though their true purpose is to keep a hunter dry, I see no reason why they can't be equally effective at keeping the sun off at least the upper portions of the body.

BEATING THE RAIN

Staying dry is a matter of finding the quietest rain gear. Follow the same in-store routine used to test the quietness of outer layers for cold weather hunting. Putting it on, walking around, pretending to draw and scratching the fabric will provide good clues as to how quietly it will perform in the deer woods.

To help keep my face dry, I wear a baseball style carbon hood under the hood of the rain gear. Because I wear glasses, keeping my face dry is more important that mere comfort. Frankly, it's difficult shooting when my glasses are sprinkled with water drops. Cleaners designed to shed water and keep glasses from fogging up may perform admirably, but their unnatural odor has always stopped me from relying on them.

As mentioned for beating the heat, stand umbrellas can also be used. Personally, I've only used them a couple of times, but have found them to perform admirably. As an added bonus, they do a better job of keeping my glasses dry than the hat trick.

Lastly, don't forget a pair of waterproof gloves. It may seem trivial, but spending hours pruning your hands isn't fun. Also, it causes them to get cold in temperatures one would normally never think of as even chilly.

CONCLUSION

Owning the right gear and knowing how to use it is great. However, you must have it with you in order to use it. I can't tell you how many times I've had a bright, sunny day called for, only to end up seeing a bank of dark clouds rolling in as I'm driving to the hunting spot. Because of that, when I'm driving any distance to reach a hunting location, I always bring my rain gear. Being a good Boy Scout and coming prepared is a huge part of winning the battle. ■

Keeping your head in the game and limiting movement, all while spending increased time in the stand, significantly improves the odds of killing a buck. That is what remaining comfortable can do for a hunter.

2. Making Equipment Work for You

I t was one of those mornings that bowhunters live for. I'd no more than gotten settled in my stand when I heard the stiff-legged walk of an approaching buck. With light slowly winning its struggle against the retreating darkness, I made out the silhouette of a young buck grunting his way toward my stand. Moments after passing, the chasing began. It was merely the beginning of the nearly nonstop action to come.

Several hours later, hearing the trotting approaching once again, I spied the nicest buck of the morning coming my way fast. His body told me it was

This wide eight-point taught me a lesson I already knew about the need to make equipment work for me.

a mature buck, but his short, dagger-like tines argued 2.5-year-old every bit as persuasively. Just as I reached for the video camera, he turned his head. In that one moment I realized the mistake I was about to make. The surprising mass of the main beams and solid 22-inch inside spread convinced me in a second that this buck was at least 3.5 years old.

Having very little time to react, I hit record and pointed the camera where I hoped the shot would occur. Acting swiftly, I twisted and grabbed my bow from its holder. Luckily for me, the buck didn't catch the speed at which I swung my body back, coming to full draw as I did so, and sent the arrow on its way. It hit low and far back. That's when I realized the tragic mistake I'd made!

As I left Bluff Country Outfitter's bunkhouse that morning, I had grabbed a new pair of gloves. I'd spent the previous afternoon moving a different stand and had sweated up the other pair to the point where I was leery of their odor.

Slipping the gloves on as I approached my stand, I noticed that I hadn't notched the inner wrist portion for my release or cut the tip of my shooting finger off. Having every intention of doing so once first light arrived, I rolled the cuff of the glove up enough to put my release on and climbed into my stand. With the nonstop action I experienced, I never had a chance to give these alterations another thought…until my arrow went slicing through the buck's lower intestines. My release was pushed more than an inch farther out from my wrist; an unnatural torque was the result.

Returning to camp, I shot four arrows before I removed the glove. The group was tight, but low and to the left—precisely the location where I had hit the buck. The next morning's tracking job was an exercise in futility. Four days later, my good friend Pat Reeves saw the buck as it slipped around a point. Eventually, I did claim the animal, but I will never forgive myself for a foolish mistake. It was one that I knew better than to make. I got lucky, but the buck that suffered needlessly didn't. That was a harsh lesson in how a hunter must make his equipment work for him. That issue is often the difference between success and failure.

FINE-TUNING MISCELLANEOUS EQUIPMENT

When most bowhunters think of tuning equipment, their thoughts migrate to their bow and arrows. I'm certainly not saying properly tuned bows and arrows aren't important. As a matter of fact, the next chapter is dedicated specifically to addressing those vital cogs. However, it's been my experience that miscellaneous gear trips up far more hunters than improperly tuned bows and arrows combined.

Let's look at that statement a little closer. First, one must understand that I'm lumping everything outside of the bow, arrows and broadheads into this group, including the improperly prepared glove that nearly cost me that buck as well as a bulky hunting jacket that can snag the string as the shot is taken.

Of course, the squeak in the tree stand that occurs as the hunter shifts position for the shot would also be factored in. So would the release that misfires. How about the frozen grunt tube that happens to produces a high-pitched squeal that scares the monster buck away. The list is seemingly endless, and I'd bet almost every reader has at least one similar horror story of his or her own.

Since almost every hunter that pursues deer uses either a tree stand or pop-up ground blind at some time, let's begin with those. The first step with both is to simply inspect them. On tree stands, it should go without saying that support cables, bolts and straps or chains must all be inspected for safety. One should also give each stand a thorough once-over to check their overall integrity. If anything is showing signs of damage, fix it before it's put to use! The hunter's safety is worth it.

The freezer provides a great testing facility for how small equipment will function in the bitter cold.

Though our lives may not depend on them, do the same checking for portable ground blinds. Pay particular attention to the cams, rods and fabric. If a rod is showing signs of wear or the fabric has a tear, you can bet it will only get worse in the field.

The next step is simply setting them up and testing them out. When testing, simulate as many acts of hunting as are practical and possible. The more paces we put the blinds through at this point, the more potential issues can be discovered.

With tree stands, after safety, the biggest issue is noise. Luckily, most often the source of unwanted noises can be dealt with. Replacing worn washers alone will often accomplish that. Along those lines, I've found that adding plastic washers between metal surfaces is a great stand-silencing technique. When neither of those actions is enough, add a lubricant to the pivot points of the stand. Though commercial lubricants last longer, I've found deer tolerate the odor of vegetable oil much better.

Finally, cinching the stand tighter onto the tree often helps. There's an effective trick that can be used on models that use the backside of the platform to leverage the stand snugly in place. After the stand has been securely strapped or chained to the tree, grab the bottom and wiggle it down as much as possible. Then, when the platform is flipped down, that baby is locked in place extra solid. Because trees naturally expand and contract, retightening is often required on stands that are left up. When one chooses to leave stands set, ALWAYS thoroughly check them before climbing in. Rodents can do a number on them in a surprisingly short time.

The act of inspecting and setting blinds before use provides the opportunity to correct issues before they are placed in the woods.

With pop-up blinds, noise can also be an issue. One of the big problems is chair squeak. When a little lubricant doesn't work, it might just be time to get a new chair. Material flap is another source of noise, as well as an unnatural visual cue to deer that something isn't right. Some of the better blinds allow for cam adjustments that effectively tighten the fabric. If that option is not available, one may either have to seam up each side or get a new blind.

With regard to fabric, pay attention to whether or not it gives off an unnatural reflection in sunlight. Frankly, I don't know of a solution for that issue. However, I do know that it spooks the heck out of deer.

Lastly, try practicing from the blind in low-light conditions. Due to the design of blinds, it gets dark inside much faster. Lighted, where legal, or top-end light-gathering pins are important. Large peep sights also help. Without either, the prime early and late shooting hours may be lost.

From these two examples, one can develop a formula for making miscellaneous hunting gear work for us. It boils down to inspection + testing + maintenance = increased hunting success.

When putting the formula to work, don't be afraid to be creative. Want to know if your grunt tube will freeze up or squeal in cold conditions? Tossing it in the freezer for a half hour will answer that. Unsure if you should drill the hole larger in a peep site? Turn off the lights in the basement and come to full draw or practice in the backyard 25 minutes after sundown. Curious about how well a piece of equipment will work in a light rain? Next time it starts sprinkling, drag it out and test it.

STORAGE

For some odd reason, storage is an all-too-often overlooked aspect of equipment care. When analyzing how each piece of equipment is stored, I look at two critical factors: Will the equipment be harmed by this storage method and will it get polluted with odors. The answers to both of those questions are equally important.

Obviously, a storage method can satisfy one of the factors without satisfying the other. A prime example is storing tree stands in the garage. If it's hung from hooks on the walls, the stand certainly won't be harmed, but it's likely to become saturated with a stink that will never leave. Vehicle exhaust and gas odors aren't the friends of hunters trying to beat a whitetail's sense of smell.

For years, I stored my tree stands outside and allowed them to weather. Though that helps ensure that odors won't be an issue, it also opens them up

Having a storage area free of foul odors goes a long ways toward making equipment work for you.

to the long-term effects of climate and rodent damage. To come up with an ideal solution, I've built a hunting shed. In it, I store all the equipment that can handle constant changes in humidity and temperatures.

My bow, arrows, optics, electronic equipment, scents and clothing are stored in the dry-storage area of my basement. Each is enclosed in a case, tub and/or plastic bag, and the storage area is kept free of noxious odor producers. For those who can't build hunting sheds, areas like this are far better locations to store hunting gear than garages can ever be. However, basement storage dictates that every item stored inside the house should be treated for odors before use.

A word of caution is in order for storing hunting clothing and other fabrics. I, like many scent-conscious hunters, store all my clothing in sealed plastic bags that are then put inside plastic tubs. This works great to keep the clothing from collecting unwanted odors, assuming that garments are put away dry. It should come as no surprise that long-term stowing of damp fabrics encourages mold and rot, so always be certain that fabrics are thoroughly dried before storing.

To help ensure that equipment will be most effective, how it's transported is also a consideration. Storing a stand in an environment free of alarming odors does little good if it's tossed in the bed of a pickup that contains gas cans, half-empty beer bottles and pools of oil. Even if it's clean, one doesn't want to subject a bow or other delicate equipment to the pounding that being tossed into the pickup bed will provide. Placing the bow in a hard case and slipping it behind the seat is a much better option. Analyzing the best method for transporting gear shouldn't be overlooked.

CONCLUSION

In a nutshell, the better our equipment is taken care of, the more exhaustive our tests and more proactively we address troublesome issues, the fewer problems we'll encounter at crunch time. Along with that, think about how the gear is stored and transported. With all of these issues addressed, our equipment is much more likely to produce the buck of a lifetime than to cause problems that cost us one. When looked at in that light, equipment care, storage and transportation suddenly aren't trivial details. They are critical to our success. ■

3. Making Your Bow Setup Sizzle

I t was the last day of season and I had a doe tag that was itching to be filled. Well before shooting light expired, a doe entered the field and began feeding. Eventually, she fed to within 70 yards. At that point, she set up camp and refused to move any closer.

With now only 10 minutes left before my season was over, and my range finder reporting her position at 50 yards and holding, I was forced to decide between taking the shot or eating the tag. As my arrow sliced through both lungs, I was pleased that I'd taken the steps required to make my bow sizzle.

Before some readers close the book in disgust at my apparent unethical decision to take that 50-yard shot, several things must be factored in. The first is that I routinely practice shooting out to 80 yards. Though I don't consider myself a great shot, repeatedly practicing at that range has resulted in my ability to consistently place those arrows in a paper plate-sized group.

To be honest, my predetermined maximum shooting range at deer has never been more than 50 yards, with the longest shot I'd previously taken being a 45-yard poke at a buck. In the cases of both the buck and doe, everything was set up perfectly. I knew the exact yardage, and the deer were frozen in place. Both shots resulted in double-lung hits and produced deer toppling within sight.

Though well over 95% of the deer I take are less than 30 yards away, the ability to reach out longer distances is one of the reasons I strive to get the most from my bow setups. The other is that, even at close ranges, every ethical advantage counts when trying to make the shot on the majestic whitetail.

SELECTING THE RIGHT BOW

More than any other piece of equipment, making your bow perform best for you begins with selecting a bow that meets your specific needs. Sure, most hunters have their favorite grunt tube and camo, but they also realize that they can take deer every bit as effectively, or close to it, with any tube or camo in the store.

That's not always the case with bows. The most glaring example of this is whether to select a bow setup that's higher on forgiveness or speed. Though each year sees the forgiveness and speed camps coming a little closer together, one of the two still comes out as the dominant player in just about every bow setup.

Deciding which is right for you requires understanding the basic concepts of each. However, keep in mind that what you are about to read are generalities. Almost every line of bows comes with its own twist that makes it at least slightly unique.

As the name implies, speed bows are geared to maximize arrow speeds. The obvious advantage is that the faster the arrow reaches its intended target, the less reaction time the animal has. For example, it would take an arrow traveling at 240 feet per second (fps), a speed considered very slow for today's compounds, 0.625 of a second to cover 50 yards, whereas it would take only 0.455 of a second for that same arrow traveling at 330 fps.

In reality, the numbers in our example are off because they don't account for arrow drag and weight, which will make the speed decrease over the arrow's flight. However, for our purposes, it illustrates the point: Though a 0.17 time difference isn't much, it can seem like eternity when dealing with an animal with lightening-fast reflexes.

As impressive as that sounds, the main advantage of speed-bow setups really lies in arrow trajectory. If identical arrows are shot under the same conditions, the faster arrow will have a flatter trajectory. That

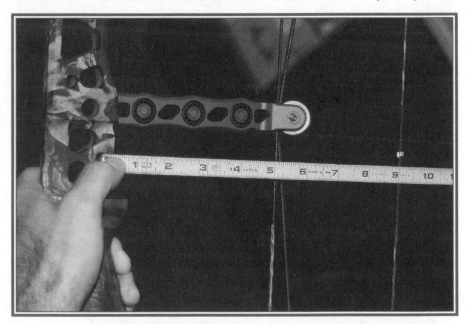

Bows with longer brace-height measurements tend to be more forgiving.

translates into speed-bow setups being more accurate on shots involving misjudged yardage estimations.

To illustrate this, let's say there's a buck standing at 35 yards and we have two hunters facing the same shot. They both go for double-lung shots by aiming half-way up the buck's body, but also incorrectly estimate the distance at 30 yards. All else being equal, one hunter is shooting a bow producing arrow speeds of 300 fps, while the other is using a setup that generates 240 fps. The likely outcome would be that the hunter shooting a bow producing arrow speeds of 300 fps would be awarded a heart shot. The 240-fps shooter would likely either graze the bottom of the buck or miss entirely. Having experienced both, I personally preferred the heart-shot result. That's the main advantage of shooting a bow that's geared for speed.

The disadvantages are that they commonly produce more noise and recoil, and they are generally more touchy. This is the result of the shorter brace heights and the more radical power strokes required to produce the fastest arrow flight. Luckily, increased noise and recoil can be somewhat minimized through the bevy of sound- and vibration-dampening products on today's market. Some of the upper-end bows even have dampening systems built directly into them.

The tougher issue is dealing with their more temperamental nature. The combination of screaming arrow speeds and reduced brace height makes maintaining proper shooting form more critical. A hitch in posture, punching the release, torturing the grip or dropping the bow arm all result in more dramatic negative effects. For most speed bows to be consistently accurate, they must be shot the proper way every time.

Though always important, properly tuning arrows and heads also becomes more important. Furthermore, many arrow and head combinations that slower, more forgiving bows handle well simply won't produce consistent results at higher speeds. In particular, many fixed-blade heads that produce large cutting diameters won't consistently group when flung at speeds approaching or exceeding 300 fps. If placed on lighter arrows, the result becomes even worse. Small cutting diameter fixed-blade and open-on-impact heads (also called expandable heads) generally fly best from speed-bow setups.

In a generalized nutshell, speed bows provide the animal with less reaction time and hit closer to the mark when the yardage estimate is off. The cost is often more noise, more recoil, an increased need for proper form and limited shooting options.

As far as forgiving bow setups are concerned, their name gives away one of their greatest advantages. Long brace heights and slower speeds translate into minimizing the sins of improper shooting form. Bows in this class are also typically longer and heavier, which makes it easier to hold steady on the target. All of that results in making them more consistently accurate at known distances. Finally, as already mentioned, they commonly produce quieter and smoother shots, and give the hunter the ability to shoot a wider range of arrows and heads that fly properly.

Aside from the disadvantages of slower arrow speeds, their increased size can also work against you. Obviously, when stalking or shooting in tight quarters, having a larger, heavier bow can be a hindrance. More space is required to swing the bow and it takes more muscle to hold it on target for as long as you can with a light bow.

Ultimately, I believe the choice between the two comes down to the hunter's experience level and hunting methods. A bow setup for speed will provide more consistent rewards to an experienced shooter who requires long-range accuracy, such as those who stalk a lot of western game. Because of their less-forgiving nature, I wouldn't recommend speed bows to those just starting out or experienced hunters who have limited practice time.

Bows set up high on the forgiveness scale are more geared toward deer hunters who spend most of their hunting time hunting in the woods, from tree stands or ground blinds. In this setting, most shots are 30 yards or less. For up-close-and-personal encounters, pulling off a quiet and accurate shot is more important than how fast the arrow gets there.

Personally, I like my setup to shoot between 270 and 280 fps. In that range, I've found the most bows that provide the best balance between noise production, speed and forgiveness, while still allowing ample options for arrows and hunting heads.

What may surprise some is the significance of arrows and heads in determining whether a bow setup leans toward speed or forgiveness. Heavy arrows, long fletchings and heavy heads all cause arrow speeds to drop. On the flip side, heavy arrows and heads increase kinetic energy. Though other factors play in, all else being equal, higher kinetic energy achieves better penetration.

BUILDING A FINELY TUNED MACHINE

With dual-cam, cam-and-a-half, single-cam and heaven only knows what's-around-the-corner cams, I'd have to commit numerous chapters to do bow tuning justice. Even then, there's no way I could do as good a job as those who tune bows for a living. My best advice is to find a local bow shop that you trust and have them ensure that your bow is a finely tuned machine. Many will even be cooperative enough to teach you about it in the process.

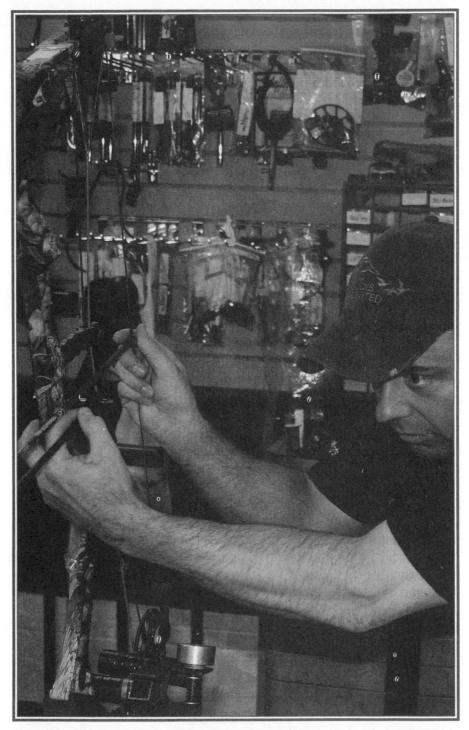

The pros who work for bow shops make their living knowing how to properly set up and tune bows. My advice is to find a good one and have him do the work for you.

With that said, there are some basic concepts that every compound shooter should grasp. The primary goal in tuning a bow is to produce arrows that fly straight. It begins with having straight arrows. However, before we address that, we have to first make sure that all the arrows are within five grams of the same weight. Heavier arrows will obviously result in low hits and lighter arrows will hit high.

Though some are gifted enough to spin arrows on tables and workbenches, I've found that I require arrow spinners to pick up the more subtle imperfections in an arrow's straightness. Furthermore, when tabletop spinning, it can be hard to determine if a wobbly arrow is due to the head or the shaft. That's why I first place arrows on the spinner without anything screwed into the insert. If any wobble occurs, the arrow goes in the trash. You simply can't get bent arrows to consistently group with straight ones.

Next, I add field points. If the field point wobbles, the insert can usually be corrected with an adjustment. Simply heat up the end of the arrow with a lighter until the glue melts just enough to twist the insert. Rotate the insert in a screwing motion and allow the glue to reset. If the spin test doesn't come out clean, keep repeating the process until it does. However, before you heat any arrow, be sure that the composition of the arrow will allow for it and that you're in a well-ventilated area.

Incidentally, it's critical to weigh hunting heads and repeat the same spin test when they are installed. I personally never worry about how the blades of fixed-blade heads align with the fletchings. So long as the head's weight is consistent, falls within the setup's ability to shoot and doesn't wobble, I've never had problems grouping heads whose blades align in every which way with the fletchings. Frankly, it's a non-issue for me. However, if I can't get an arrow and head combination to spin clean, I won't shoot it.

As mentioned at the beginning of this section, I will assume that the bow has already been tuned. Issues such as timing, tilter measurements and such are already adjusted properly. However, one must realize that strings and cables stretch over time and shots. As they do, the bow will again require tuning. Marking the point where the string leaves the cam or wheel groove is one method of keeping track. Another is to mark the cam or wheel positions relative to the limbs. Either way works and creates a quick reference point to check for string stretch or other issues that will require tuning.

Though I recommend having pros tune readers' bows, I do believe that it's important for bowhunters to understand the basics of setting up a bow. Frankly, if a hunter goes on a remote trip or simply doesn't have

Regularly waxing the string is an easy way to prolong its life.

a shop nearby, basic knowledge and preparedness is enough to conquer many equipment problems.

A well-shooting bow begins with a properly set nock. The nock should be placed so that the bottom of the arrow nock is 1/8th inch above 90 degrees. Being a smidge higher won't hurt, but being too low can cause problems with the arrow contacting the bow.

Next, the center shot should be adjusted. Center shot refers to how the arrow is aligned in relationship to the string and riser. Many easy-to-use center-shot tools are available to adjust the rest. Most mount on the outside of the riser and adjust until they're centered on the string. Then, either the marked point or the laser is flipped over to the arrow. From that, by aligning the centering tool to the string and creating a reference point, one can see if the rest must be adjusted right or left to center the arrow.

If the center shot is slightly off, it doesn't have tremendous effect on accuracy. However, the results are noticeable when arrows shot at different yardages migrate to the left or right. For example, assuming all the pins are set in identical right and left positions, if the shooter is dead on at 20 yards, but the 40-yard groups are to the left of the bull's-eye, the center shot is off. It requires adjusting the rest to the right to bring these groups back into proper alignment. The opposite is true for left-handed shooters.

With that out of the way, focus on making sure the fletchings are clearing the rest. If they don't, some form of a bump will occur. Because not every fletching is identical, that will cause groups to become larger. I've found that marking the fletchings with white lipstick works very well for this. Rotate the arrows' nocks until you find the magic spot where they fly without leaving marks behind on the rest or riser.

That often doesn't work with radical helical-fletched arrows that are being shot from stationary rests, or if the nocking point is so low that the arrow is driven down to contact the bow. In the first case, either switching to straighter fletchings or a drop-away rest can solve the problem. In the case of a low nocking point, simply raise the nock up the string until the arrow clears.

As a side note, I believe that the string is the most overlooked aspect of bow maintenance. Nothing stops a bow from being able to perform any more effectively than a broken string. Wax is cheap. Waxing the string once for every month of shooting is fast, easy and can save the hunter from a headache that could have been avoided.

Though not an end-all source of information on setting up or tuning bows, the information in this section should be sufficient to get hunters through many equipment issues and back on their feet. In most cases, having this information, as well as some basic tools, will be enough to get the bow back to the point that it can be sighted in. Sure, it probably won't be perfectly tuned, but it should be close enough to shoot consistent groups and get you through until it can be fine-tuned.

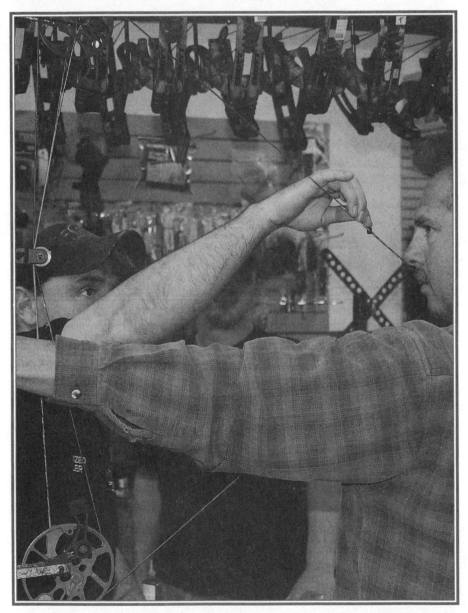

After the first 100 shots with a new string, the plastic tubing can be removed from the peep sight by adjusting the peep's orientation on the string and training it to naturally align at full draw.

A piece of felt or moleskin placed on the rest removes the noise generated by the arrow being dragged across it.

SILENCING THE BOW

Thus far, we've focused on what kind of bow to buy and how to make it shoot well. Regardless of how fast or slow the bow may be, making it shoot quietly is vital. The reason is simple: Bow noise is what most often causes deer to jump the string.

As already mentioned, adding commercial sound and vibration dampeners is a good step. These are available as products that attach to the limbs or are built into stabilizers, and there's always the old standby of the group that slips into the string. Each one can do a little more to hush the shot. Remember, there's no such thing as a bow being too quiet.

Next, get rid of the plastic tubing that aligns the peep sight. The slap sound it generates is simply unacceptable, in my opinion. It can be eliminated by either switching to a self-aligning peep or training the string, so those designed for use with tubing will come back properly aligned without it.

The first step toward continued use of peeps that require tubing involves shooting the first 100 arrows from bows with new strings. On new strings, some degree of stretching is very common. After around the first 100 shots, good strings settle and become stable. Removing the rubber tubing before that point doesn't serve much of a purpose. As a side note, because of the string stretch, it's a good idea to fine-tune the bow again after the first 100 shots.

With the tubing removed, slap the bow on a bow press and orient the peep to a position that brings it close to coming to proper alignment naturally at full draw. To fine-tune it, experiment to find the orientation the peep must have before coming to full draw, so that it ultimately aligns properly when pulled back. Next, simply twist the peep to that position before drawing the bow. After doing that before each shot, over a handful of practice sessions, the string becomes trained and the peep naturally maintains alignment.

However, it's still a good idea to remember how the peep must set naturally in the string and check it at the beginning of each hunt. I personally glance at it each time I nock an arrow. Then, when hunting, either at first light or right after I settle into the stand for an afternoon hunt, I come to full draw once to ensure that I'm good to go. If the peep is slightly off, let down the draw and twist the string to position it properly.

With those steps out of the way, it's time to focus on the rest. I've found that the plastic products commonly applied to the areas where the arrow contacts the rest produce too much noise on still mornings. To fix that, replace the plastic covering with either felt or mole's skin. On drop-away rests that hit metal or plastic when in their down position, also cover that area to deaden the noise.

Lastly, thoroughly inspect the bow and accessories for any loose pieces. Tightening them will reduce sound-producing vibrations. With that, we now have created a silent killing machine.

CONCLUSION

Unlike when I was a kid, I'm not sure there's still such a thing as poorly built bows. Technologies have come so far and the bow market is so competitive that if a company came out with a real dud, it'd likely go belly-up swiftly. That puts archers in a much better place than they were even just 10 years ago.

Now, instead of worrying about getting a good bow, we can focus on getting one that best suits our needs. Once the field has been narrowed to the bows that meet our desires, shoot them and go with the one that produces consistent groups and feels best in your hand.

Next, outfit the setup with the appropriate arrows, heads and accessories that either work toward your goals for what you want from your bow or minimize its negative side effects. When doing so, remember that the bow will never perform better than the arrows will allow. Having straight, well-balanced arrows that spin clean will allow the bow setup to achieve its potential.

Finally, find someone you trust to help fine-tune the bow to its maximum potential. If hunters are willing to spend big dollars on bows, it doesn't make sense for most to save $20 by setting it up themselves. However, to minimize the risks of hunts being ruined by equipment issues, everyone should have some basic bow-setup skills, as well as the required tools and parts. With all that, you can have a bow that performs at levels unheard of in years past. ■

Spinning arrows is essential to ensure that they are straight and the heads are aligned properly.

4. The Formula for Beating a Whitetail's Nose

Having constructed a mock scrape earlier, I knew there was at least one mature buck working the area. The flurry of buck sign that appeared, as a reaction to the dominant-buck urine in the mock scrape, left no doubt about that. I'd been waiting for the right phase of season and wind direction to hunt this particular stand. The setup was a funnel leading into a family group bedding area. When the wind direction

Bucks like this one are what make going the extra mile to reduce odors worth the effort.

resulted in the funnel being downwind of the bedding area, it became an ideal location for intercepting cruising bucks.

Finally, with breeding activity ready to explode any day, the wind cooperated. As I laid my scent trail, I purposefully dragged it over the mock scrape I was covering. My confidence soared even higher when I saw the massive track of the buck that had recently worked it. As I climbed into my stand, I couldn't help but believe this was my day.

After several hours of watching squirrels, a small front rolled in. Unexpected fronts and switching winds are just some of the reasons I take odor reduction so seriously. Though the wind shifted with the front and was now blowing directly into the bedding area, I remained confident that my odor stream would go undetected. My only concern was that the new wind could shift the majority of the cruising activity to the other side of the bedding area.

Mere moments later, I heard the first grunt coming from the bedding area. Slowly turning in that direction, I saw him. He was following the scent trail with his nose to the ground, and it took only one glance to see he was the shooter I was after.

My heart sank as he stopped in the exact spot where the breeze detector indicated he would intersect any unwanted odors. As he slowly raised his head, I couldn't help but question whether my odor-reduction techniques had failed me and were about to foil an otherwise perfect event. The relief I felt as he turned his head to watch a doe mill behind him was tremendous. He horseshoed his body just enough to provide a broadside shot at his vitals as he watched the doe, and I let the arrow fly. I watched him drop after running a 40-yard buttonhook route. My odor-reduction techniques had produced yet another buck.

CAN A BUCK'S NOSE BE DEFEATED?

When bowhunting deer, there are certain givens. You can't shoot a 150-inch buck if one never sets foot on your hunting property, you can't legally take deer from the living room couch, and you can't beat a white-tail's nose.

Though I completely agree with the first two statements, I have no doubt in my mind that the third is untrue. I know that because I couldn't even begin to tell you how many hundreds of deer I've had downwind that never had a clue I was there!

Having experimented with smoke machines, I'll be the first to admit that wind flow isn't always what it may appear. Often, the breeze will carry smoke out several yards, only to have it hook to the right, left, up or down. Because of that, I'm confident that there have been many occasions when hunters believed deer were in their odor stream, only to be mistaken.

As it applies to picking up human odors, a deer's sense of smell is so far advanced from ours that we can't even begin to grasp its power. That alone makes me question if the odor stream didn't take an unexpected jog, completely avoiding the deer's nose and tricking the hunter into believing he defeated the animal's sense of smell.

However, when hunters experience calm deer seemingly downwind from their position time and time again, I become a believer. That's what happens to me on at least a weekly basis during hunting season. Though I don't mention it often in writing, except while hunting late season, I rarely pass on a stand site just because the wind will blow toward approaching deer. As a matter of fact, as you will read in a later chapter, I often set stands knowing that deer will approach from downwind!

Does that mean I believe my techniques destroy all human odors? No way! The body is an odor-producing machine whose assembly line of aromas can't reasonably ever be completely shut down. But odor production can be slowed and minimized so that it isn't an issue.

Though we will never truly know why until we learn to talk to deer, I believe one of two things can be achieved: The first possibility is that odor will be minimized to the point that the source appears to be a great distance away, instead of in the tree 15 yards away. The other is that odor can be reduced so that it diffuses before it reaches the whitetail's nose. It is so weak that the deer doesn't pick it up.

Which is it? I don't know. I just know that it's possible to beat a whitetail's nose through most of season.

The exception to this is when hunting the upper Midwest and northern regions of the whitetail's range during the late season and second rut phase. In most of that region, firearms season will have already come and gone. Having lived through the war, the remaining deer are true survivors and ultra skittish. Along with that, almost all plant life is either dead, dormant, frozen or in a combination of these states. The result is that very few natural odors are left to cover your scents. Furthermore, the relative lack of leaves and tall weeds creates fewer odor-diffusing barriers between the hunter and the deer.

All of that makes going unscented a far more difficult proposition. In fact, though I can count on my fingers the times I know I was winded in the last nine years before those stages of season, I will get pegged by approximately 50% of the mature deer that get downwind of me during these last two phases of season. Of those that pick me up, around half get a smidge nervous but carry on normally. The other half blow out of there as if their lives depended on it. Because of that, after the breeding phase of the season concludes, I religiously hunt stands downwind of where I believe deer will pass.

Because the wind direction isn't a constant, the author believes that employing a thorough scent-reduction strategy is a better than relying on staying downwind of deer.

DIFFERENT STROKES

One more item must be addressed before we get into how to beat a whitetail's nose. I firmly believe that different tactics and approaches work better for some than others. A handful of very serious hunting friends that I trust implicitly don't do anywhere near as much as I do to defeat a whitetail's nose. Yet they pay no attention to the wind and claim they're almost never winded.

On the flip side, Jim Hill, an extremely serious Minnesota hunter, takes some things well beyond what I do and would be the first to admit that he doesn't go undetected every time. I have a cousin that does nearly everything by the odor-reduction book, but routinely gets winded.

My point is that some of you may be able to get away with less than I do and be fine. Others may have to go beyond and still have issues. My scent-reduction strategy works for my cameramen and me. Nearly every new cameraman I get groans when he sees the list of scent rules he must follow. Most admit later that they thought it was a waste of time, but our consistent results changed their minds.

I can't guarantee the same results for everyone. What I can guarantee is that I believe in this system. I also am extremely confident in saying that it has allowed me to effectively alter my strategies, and it has delivered far more bucks to my walls than I'd ever had if I didn't follow this system so rigorously.

TREATING CLOTHES, THE BODY AND BREATH

From the pictures scattered throughout this book, it should be readily apparent that I depend on Scent-Lok and Wildlife Research Center's scent-killing products. Since they both come with pretty straightforward instructions on proper use, I will cover them very briefly here.

First, regardless of what carbon suit is used, it's important to understand that it can't differentiate between good and bad odors. Carbon suits work like a sponge in that they trap odors inside. They also share another similarity: they can only trap so much. After saturation occurs, a sponge can't hold more water and a carbon suit can't trap more odors. At that point, until wrung out, they are both worthless. From that, one should be able to understand that applying cover scent directly to the suit or storing it with pine bows are self-defeating acts. All they do is saturate the suit faster so that threatening odors can escape.

As far as Scent Killer is concerned, and I believe this is true of most competing brands as well, it works by not allowing odors to form. Additionally, it works equally well when dried and will continue to

Once hunting clothing has been treated, ensuring that it remains scent free is critical.

perform until it has either flaked off or has exhausted itself through altering odor molecules. Because of that, I spray my under layers after washing and drying. So long as they will be used within a month of treatment and don't become contaminated, they won't need to be sprayed again until after they are used.

I am working under the assumption that everyone reading this understands that one must wash every under layer that will be used, both while traveling to the hunting site and while hunting, as well as washcloths and towels. Obviously, a scent-free detergent is the best bet, but in a pinch, baking soda will also work.

Line drying the clothing is preferred. If that isn't an option, or your neighborhood doesn't have good air quality, be certain to clean the dryer to the best of your ability before tossing your treated hunting clothing inside. Along those lines, also be sure to wash your hands in scent-free soap before handling treated clothing.

Once dried, spray the clothing down with a scent-killing spray and hang to dry. For this step, if hanging outside isn't an option, choose the most odor-free room in the house and rig a hanging system. As soon as the clothing is dry to the touch, store it in a clean, airtight container until ready for use.

As far as containers are concerned, I go with a two-layered approach. First, all treated clothing goes inside an unscented garbage bag. To remove their plastic odors, new bags are hung on the line and sprayed down with a hose. After a week or so has passed, they are turned inside out, sprayed down again and allowed to hang for another week.

The clothes-filled bags are then stored in ScenTote containers. Though sealed tubs can work, even if one can find airtight tubs, a ScenTote container has advantages. Its first nice feature is that the 20-gallon tote is truly airtight. Next, mounted to the inside of the lid is an Activated Carbon-Web Adsorber, and a Carbon-Web Adsorber Pocket, designed to store and de-scent smaller items, mounts to the side. The Carbon-Webs continuously release activated carbon granules to capture scent, and like carbon suits, they're recharged from 30 minutes in the drier. This product has the potential to truly keep scent-free items pure, as well as to help de-scent contaminated objects.

When it comes to the body, it should be a given that showers are taken with scent-free soaps and shampoos before each trip into the woods. With that said, one of the places many hunters trip up occurs as they step out of the shower. They've just thoroughly scrubbed every inch of their body, and then they reach for a towel. It's the same towel that their mother, wife, girlfriend or even they themselves washed and dried . . . using some scented detergent and a fragrant fabric-softener sheet in the dryer.

So now, there they are, rubbing perfume odors all over their glistening skin and dripping hair, effectively counteracting any benefit from the shower. As silly as it may sound, you may be shocked at how many people do just that!

My only other further comment on body care is that I strongly recommend that all use of scented deodorants, shampoos, soaps and aftershaves be stopped a full month before season begins. The hair and pores become saturated with these perfumed odors. By switching over to scent-free alternatives in advance of season, the hair and pores have an opportunity to cleanse themselves.

For breath care, I avoid eating and drinking strong-smelling foods and liquids. As much as many may hate to hear this, that means coffee is not an option. Regardless of how thoroughly you brush your teeth and gargle, that coffee smell simply won't leave your throat.

Speaking of brushing teeth, I brush my teeth with Arm & Hammer's unflavored baking soda toothpaste. When doing so, I pay extra attention to brushing both the top and bottom of my tongue, gums and the roof of my mouth. Then I finish up by gargling with Hawgs Limited's Vanishing Hunter. It is some of the most vile-tasting liquid that one can ever put in the mouth, but it also kills odors like nothing else I've tried.

LOOKING AT EQUIPMENT

Many hunters do at least some of those things to care for their body, breath and clothes, only to still get tripped up by overlooking the seemingly little details. Deer could care less if they are winding the hunter, the stand, the bow or anything else brought into the woods. All they know is that their nose has told them something is wrong, and they need to be heading the other way fast.

Maybe your release stinks! Think about it. What gets sweatier more than the wristband of a release? We use them all summer long and practice using them during season. All the while, bacteria are thriving and producing their noxious odors. Then we shower, slap on our hunting gear, grab our release and head into the woods. As the deer snorts and torpedoes in the other direction, we curse our scent-eliminating products, never considering that we are wearing a stinky release. That could just as easily be our calls, knives, safety harnesses, sandwiches, or any other objects we're carrying.

My first step in avoiding these potentially hunt-ruining traps is to take inventory of every item I am bringing into the woods. When doing so, I analyze if I really need it. For example, I don't really have to bring my wallet, but I find a watch and my glasses indispensable. So the wallet stays home and my glasses and watch are washed in hydrogen peroxide each time before I head out. When it applies to knives, drag ropes or any other post-success tools, I leave them in the truck for retrieval when necessary.

Whenever practical, the items that go into the woods with me are used exclusively in the woods. That makes keeping them odor free an easier task. I have a watch that I only wear for hunting. I also have two releases that are identical in every way, except that one has a large X on the wrist and is used exclusively for practice. The other, outside of being shot once before season begins to ensure reliability, is used only for hunting.

Furthermore, all of my equipment is treated. My bow case has a tight seal, and its inside is washed several times during season, along with being sprayed down with Scent Killer once a week. I also I wipe down my bow, arrows and even my broadheads with a hydrogen peroxide-soaked paper towel at least once every two weeks during season.

My two pairs of rubber boots and Elimitrax are washed weekly, both inside and out, with a mixture of scent-free liquid soap and water. After drying outside, they are ready for use. If it will be a while between uses, I dump about a cup of baking soda in them and store them in a sealed container.

As a side note, new rubber boots smell. To combat that, purchase boots a year in advance and treat them once a month before use. That will help rid them of odors.

The point I'm trying to make is that our efforts and supporting products will only go as far as we let them. To be able to get by the nose of a whitetail, any and everything we bring with us must be treated. All of my hunting gear is washed once a week, either in a combination scent-free soap and water or hydrogen peroxide, then sealed until it's needed and sprayed down right before heading into the woods. Remember, your calls, rattling antlers, optics and every other piece of gear must be addressed.

FINAL TOUCHES

In addition to those things, we must address our vehicles. It should go without saying that we never wear our boots or hunting clothing in the truck. Personally, I wear treated clothing to my parking location, only to shed it and put on fresh under layers. Also, when I am depending on it for hunting, I try to clean the truck's interior at least once a week. Even with that, I lay down plastic bags on the seat and keep the windows down as I drive. I seldom use ATVs, but when I do, I wear a rain suit to minimize contamination.

We must get to the stand without leaving an odor trail, and Elimitrax allow me to do that. They are much like hip boots that are put on over the hunting boot. Their fabric is specially designed not to give off any odor.

However, I still believe that mature animals get jumpy when they run across the freshly crushed twigs, leaves and grasses left as we pass through. These are natural odors, but so is the odor of what left these smells. When a cagey old buck can't pinpoint the maker of such a trail, I believe it puts him on edge. That is why I use boot pads that are laced with non-estrus doe urine or immature, non-rutting buck urine. I have yet to see an animal spook when he hits that trail. One sniff and they conclude that a doe walked through. As a beneficial side effect, the smell of deer urine helps to calm deer and assure them that the area is safe.

When not wearing Elimitrax, I slap the urine-laced boot pads on my rubber boots. Between staying clean, being sprayed down and applying the deer urine, I also have excellent success with this method. Where it can fail is when the pant legs brush against objects. Despite everything I do, I've actually watched deer sniff the grass I brushed against, turn

Selecting a location to change upwind of the truck is an important step in remaining scent free.

Spraying down after changing and again when settled in the stand helps defeat freshly forming odors.

around, and walk back in the direction they came. Because Elimitrax are worn up to the hip, they make it easier to slip through tall grass without leaving odors behind.

Lastly, we must minimize scent on stand. That begins with dressing light and going slow on the approach. Once there, extra layers can be added. This is a good time to spray down high-perspiration areas. I also carry a pack of paper towels that were soaked in scent-killing spray to wipe my exposed skin down with. My drink of choice is water and I only bring apples to eat. Even then, every couple of hours I gargle again with Vanishing Hunter. With all that, I am confident that I can beat a mature buck's nose.

CONCLUSION

As you can see, employing my odor-reduction techniques isn't a quick or painless process. For me, beating a whitetail's nose requires a dedicated, thorough and consistent approach. During the course of the season, I may only get one or two chances at trophy bucks. I do everything reasonably within my power to ensure that my odors don't foil those opportunities. Since perfecting this process, my shot opportunities have increased many times over. For me, that makes it easily worth-while.

With that said, I feel compelled to remind the readers that hunting is supposed to be fun. If taking all these steps removes the enjoyment of the hunt for you, then don't do it. Sometimes, we tend to lose focus on purely enjoying the sport. Personally, if I didn't take these steps, I'd become so bothered by switching and swirling winds that the fun would be drained from the hunt. Find the balance for yourself and enjoy hunting to the fullest. ■

5. Stand Placement: 7 Steps to Staying in Bucks All Season

As beneficial as learning how to combat odor has been in delivering shot opportunities, developing a strategy for stand placement during the various phases of the season has been every bit as critical for putting me in the right position. I feel so strongly about this that half of my first book, *Advanced Stand Hunting Strategies*, is dedicated to nothing else.

When you really break it down, a mature buck and his habitat go through many changes over the course of a season. It should come as no surprise to students of trophy bucks that changing testosterone levels trigger many of the significant behaviors and processes these animals endure. In chronological order, the testosterone's rise and eventual fall prompts velvet shedding and increased aggression, serves as a priming mechanism for rubbing and scraping, becomes a factor in increased daylight movement, and, ultimately, causes the eventual shedding of the antlers. Of course, one must also factor the estrous cycles of does and the presence of fawns into the equation. All of that results in some serious changes in a buck's life.

The deer's habitat goes through many changes as well, transforming from a relatively lush bounty that provides protective cover to a setting that is comparatively barren. As you will find in the following chapter, food sources are also undergoing massive changes in both desirability and availability.

Once one begins grasping all of the changes that occur over a hunting season, it becomes easy to understand that a buck's wants, needs and desires also change. Not coincidentally, his general patterns shift with these changes. Because of that, it only makes sense to change our hunting strategies to mirror these facts.

Effectively doing this really boils down to answering what drives bucks during the season. From that, we can see seven distinct phases of season: early season, the October lull, peak scrape phase, chase phase, breeding phase, second rut and post rut. With that understanding, we can devise precise strategies for each phase that maximize the hunter's odds by focusing on what bucks want and need.

EARLY-SEASON SUCCESS

To begin the season, bucks are living a pretty good life. Food sources and cover are plentiful. Depending on the date of the opener, bucks are either experiencing the tail end of their bachelor grouping days or have just recently disbanded. Either way, though a loose pecking order has already been established, the all-out battles for position within the buck hierarchy and breeding rights are still to come. All in all, it's a pretty good time to be a mature buck.

Buck patterns change with the phases of season. To keep yourself in mature bucks all season long, you must change with them.

During this phase of season, consisting of approximately the first two weeks after the opener, food, water, safety and comfort are the bucks' top priorities. Because they haven't had to worry about man much yet, many still feel relatively safe moving during late-afternoon hours. All of this makes targeting a mature buck's food and water sources a good choice.

Obviously, a critical component in pulling that off is finding at least one mature buck to target. Early-season success is all about nailing a buck's route between bedding and food and water. Unlike during the rut, bucks won't be covering much ground. If you aren't keyed into their patterns, the odds of success plummet. Observations and scouting cameras performing surveillance on selected foods and water sources are tremendous aids.

When employing either, you have three goals. Obviously, the first is to make sure a shooter is present. Next, pinpointing his trail is key. All too often, one close call is all a hunter can hope for. Blowing it by guessing and setting up on a trail upwind of the buck's entrance route almost always equals failure for hunters who don't take odor control to the extreme. Last, finding and documenting his track can be extremely beneficial. Though we will cover these scouting techniques in detail in Chapter 9, it's important to mention them now so you can begin to understand how they can be put to productive use.

Though nailing the early-season patterns of one buck is a good start, it's always best to have backups. My goal each season is to have the patterns of three separate bucks nailed for early season. I've found that having three allows me to shift between them enough to keep each buck off guard and my stands fresh. Along with that, it provides a safety blanket for when something unexpected ruins the best-laid plans on one or two of these bucks.

At this point, I'm sure many readers are thinking that it's impossible for them to pattern three mature bucks. I also wouldn't be surprised if some believe the only reason I can is because I'm a spoiled writer with sole access to endless acres of prime hunting lands. As much as I wish this were the case, I can honestly say that it isn't. I'm blessed to work as a consultant for some of the top outfitters, and I do receive the right to hunt as partial payment. However, their clients always come first.

I begin the hunting season in my home state of Wisconsin each year, with every intention of filling that buck tag before moving on to other states. I'm extremely lucky to work with Tom Indrebo who, along with his wife, Laurie, owns and operates Bluff Country Outfitters in trophy rich Buffalo County. One of the three bucks I strive to pattern does come from their lands.

The other two are almost always on Wisconsin's heavily hunted public lands. It shouldn't come as a surprise that most hunters don't believe mature bucks exist in such areas. I'm here to tell you that they do in more cases than not. I also have firsthand knowledge that it's the same for public lands in Minnesota, Michigan, Iowa, Illinois, Kansas, Missouri and Alberta, Canada. Though I haven't hunted public lands in other regions of the whitetail's range, I do know hunters who have unearthed mature bucks on public lands in most states and provinces. In other words, if you're willing to put in the work and some miles on the truck, I feel confident that the majority of readers are capable of patterning three mature bucks. However, just like me, most will also have to compete with other hunters on public lands to accomplish that.

Particularly around bedding areas, stand sites should be prepared well before season begins.

Another consideration is that I want to be done patterning these bucks and have stands prepared a full week before season begins, which provides a little time for the woods to settle down. However, concluding your observations and stand prep much before that time increases the risk that the buck's patterns may naturally change before season begins.

When determining stand sites, a balance must be struck between getting within bow range and staying undetected. So long as the buck doesn't bust the hunter, the battle continues. Once busted, the war is almost always over. Because of that, I take an outside approach, focusing my hunting on the fringes of a buck's core area and only moving in when necessary.

Even when focusing on the outside, one should only hunt stands that offer the best access and lowest odds of disturbing the buck. Obviously, for most hunters, that includes only hunting stands with the right wind. Because of the low impact they typically provide, sitting stands on food and water sources qualifies as a productive way of hunting from the outside.

The risk of using these stands is that the hunter had better be prepared to stay pinned in the tree until after dark. Crawling down before, a sea of eyes will effectively blow the deal, even if Mr. Big isn't amongst them.

A stand placed just off of the food source, back in the woods where the trail splits or is intersected by a crossing trail, is another good choice. Being 20-50 yards back in is often enough to catch bucks during the last few minutes of legal hours. The price is that the hunter loses the possibility of selecting the wrong trail, but still having a monarch feed its way into range.

The choice should ultimately be made according to which placement is least intrusive and still provides maximum odds of a daylight encounter. With all of that in place, early season can be a great time to arrow a mature buck!

BEATING THE OCTOBER LULL

Unfortunately, in most areas receiving pressure, daylight sightings on the food and water sources dry up after the first couple weeks of season. In many areas, this is also about the same time that leaves begin dropping. The combination of hunting pressure and the sudden nakedness of the woods drives many mature bucks toward a more nocturnal lifestyle.

I believe the approaching breeding phase further inspires this. Between fighting, chasing does and breeding, bucks burn more energy during that phase than in any other. At the same time, feeding activity is often dramatically reduced. The net result is the need to build a thick layer of fat to serve as energy reserves for the approaching breeding phase. Reducing movement by spending the daylight hours lounging in bed and gorging themselves during the dark hours is the avenue many mature bucks use to build the impressive fat layers they will soon rely on.

Because of all this, it's often necessary to get close to a buck's bedding area to realize daylight movement. The mission is to set up along the buck's path to food, as close to his bed as is reasonably possible, without him knowing you're there.

A big part of that is getting in and out unnoticed. Remember, if all plays out the way we hope, the buck will be in that bed when we slip in for our afternoon hunt. If he catches us, the jig is up.

There really isn't a cut-and-dried answer to how close we can get. Many factors, such as wind direction, topography, the buck's ability to see approaching danger, the noise made entering the stand and the hunter's own skill at slipping undetected through the woods, all work together to decide what this distance is.

Complicating matters is that we want to get it right the first time. Bucks are very in tune to the territory close to their bedding areas. Even when we keep trimming activities and other disturbances to a minimum, chances are it's asking too much to get away with adjusting stand locations around the buck's bedding area. Ideally, the stand should be prepped before season and left alone.

Ultimately, the precise placement becomes a balance between being close enough to realize daylight movement, the amount of noise that will be made getting in, the buck's ability to see from his bed, and each hunter's ability to remain undetected. As with many things in hunting, allow common sense and woodsmanship to be your guides. Do that, and the October lull can be beaten!

SCRAPING UP BUCKS

As challenging as the lull can be, it also serves as the doorway to the peak scraping phase. Now is when things start getting to be really fun for those who have done their homework.

At this point, building testosterone levels are really starting to show their effect. With breeding time approaching, bucks want to firmly establish their position in the hierarchy and advertise their presence. Because of that, fresh scrapes and rubs are now appearing daily.

Scrapes are now great places to hunt, but there are hurdles to doing so effectively. One of them is that a mature buck can make over 200 scrapes during a season. Of these, he tends a relatively low percentage on a consistent basis. Furthermore, though his daylight movements are now on the rise, most of his scraping activities will still occur at night. Ultimately, successful scrape-hunting techniques boil down to proper timing, targeting scrapes that are consistently used by mature bucks during daylight hours, and keeping bucks ignorant of the fact that they're being hunted.

By the beginning of the peak scraping phase, bucks are really starting to feel the effects of their rising testosterone levels.

The timing factor is important because if hot scrapes are hunted too early, chances are good that the bucks working them are still predominately nocturnal. Under those conditions, the most likely outcome is that the bucks will be educated and abandon the scrapes before the hunter has a fighting chance. On the flip side, once the chase phase begins, mature bucks are way too focused on finding does to worry about regularly tending even their hottest scrapes.

I've found hunting scrapes to be the best during the 12-day period before the chase phase begins. In most of the upper Midwest, that translates to the last five days of October and the first seven days of November. In other areas, backing up from the peak breeding date by three weeks is a good starting point.

Next, one must find the right scrapes to target. The best route to uncovering consistently worked scrapes comes through spring scouting. Because scrapes are whitetails' equivalent of billboards, it only makes sense that the most effective advertising will be located in areas where deer activities are concentrated. Provided that drastic changes don't occur in deer patterns or habitat, those locations remain the same year after year, and so do the sites of the most productive scrapes.

Finding scrapes in the spring provides the opportunity to gauge the level of use they received. Simply put, scrapes with a deep bowled-out shape or overly exaggerated ovals of dirt accurately reveal that they were worked the most consistently last fall. Because of the likelihood that they will be used heavily again, it's a very good bet that they will be hot scrapes again during the coming season.

If spring scouting simply isn't an option, the task becomes harder, but certainly not impossible. Mid-October scouting trips reveal many scrapes. The trick is determining which ones are being used most heavily. Performing these in-season scouts during mid-day hours helps minimize disturbances.

Once the area's consistently worked scrapes have been found, one must then target the scrapes most likely to be used during daylight. Though field-edge scrapes often look impressive, scrapes located back in the woods or in secluded openings are better choices. The feeling of safety these areas provide can be enough to entice a buck to visit during daylight. Scrapes located near a buck's bedding area also provide better odds of intercepting him during daylight, as he slips into his bedroom after a late night or decides to get up a little earlier in the afternoon. Finally, scrapes positioned on the downwind sides of doe-bedding areas are good choices.

Stand location is an important consideration. Because many mature bucks check scrapes by skirting them on the downwind side, a lot of stands that cover scrapes allow many bucks to slip through outside of bow range.

Personally, I've always had the best luck by placing stands about 20 yards away on the prevailing wind's downwind side of the scrape. Doing this not only allows me to cover the scrape, but also to cover the bucks that are slipping by as much as 50 yards downwind. I have found that such positioning produces more shot opportunities than any other. Following those guidelines can produce fantastic results.

BEATING THE CHASE

As the scrape phase draws to a close, the insanity begins. With a handful of early does already bred and more does being on the cusp of readiness, mature bucks now seem to lose their composure. It's almost as if they can't resist checking every doe they can find. If she is close, you can bet they'll chase her all around the woods. Heck, they'll often even dog does that are over a week or more away from being ready to breed.

For as much fun as the bucks seem to have, does that are not ready for breeding appear not to want to have anything to do with their games. They often head for the thickest cover they can find and run circles through it, trying to lose their pursuers. Often, the chase doesn't end until either she loses the bucks in the cover or they tire of her and go off to find another doe and repeat the process.

Two stand placements work very well during this phase. The first is stands placed in funnels separating doe concentrations. Because bucks are going from doe concentration to doe concentration, their travels will likely involve using these funnels.

The next effective placement is slapping stands in the thickest cover the area provides. In this case, it's best to pick trees that are on the downwind edge of the cover and that offer the best concealment. Because the doe is likely to run all over the cover, providing shot opportunities in unpredictable locations, I've found that going undetected is a better strategy than setting up where the most sign can be covered. Chances are every bit as good she'll lead them by there as anywhere else.

Another consideration is that in this situation, numerous shooting lanes are a must. When trying to arrow a buck chasing a doe, the chances of things occurring in an orderly fashion are almost nonexistent.

Balancing your need for numerous shooting lanes with your ability to refrain from clear-cutting the cover will tilt the odds toward the buck eventually stopping in an opening. Setting up on the edge of the thicket means half of the stand-coverage area will require less trimming to create shooting lanes. Still, because of the overall level of trimming required, it's best to prepare these stand sites well before season begins. When in the right place at the right time, this brief, five-day or so phase can result in literally having a parade of bucks pass the stand.

BRINGING ORDER TO THE BREEDING CHAOS

Obviously, the chase phase signals that breeding time has nearly arrived. I've always found it rather ironic that so many hunters are convinced that the breeding phase offers their best chance of arrowing Mr. Big. Frankly, I've long believed that this is the phase that requires more luck than any other.

The idea of patterning a specific buck now has been thrown out the window. During the breeding phase, most mature bucks dramatically expand their home ranges, with a percentage abandoning them altogether. Simply put, they are putting on the miles in search of hot does. Once she's found, he will try to corral her off in an area where he can have her all to himself. If she resists his lead, he will follow her anywhere she wants to go. In other words, his patterns have been thrown out the window.

Understanding what a buck wants and how he gets it is the key to bringing order to this chaos. Mature bucks want to find a steady supply of hot does. To accomplish this, they must check the locations where does concentrate. Additionally, bucks need to do that in ways that expend the least amount of effort and provide the greatest safety.

Strategically positioned topographical funnels help them save energy and feel safe, offering the easiest route through otherwise challenging terrain.

For example, if there's a saddle in a steep ridge, it gives bucks that want to cross over the ridge an energy-saving option. By choosing to cross at the low spot, they're able to save gas for their doe-finding road trip. The steeper the ridge and lower the saddle, the more inviting that route becomes to the bucks. When a saddle separates two doe concentrations or food sources and doe-bedding areas, it can be a great setup.

Habitat funnels most often address the safety factor. To illustrate this, picture two square blocks of timber surrounded by open farm fields. Now, add a brush-choked fence line connecting them. After checking the does in one block, the buck can make a death run across the open field or travel the fence line's cover to the other timber. Unless previously educated by brushes with hunters in the funnel, the route with cover will appear much safer.

The best funnels are those that seem to be the easiest and safest routes to where bucks want to go. During the rut, funnels separating deer concentrations often result in the best stands available.

Another tactic that plays to rutting bucks' weaknesses is hunting doe-bedding areas. These are great places for bucks to find receptive does. That makes them great places for hunters to score.

Bucks commonly rely on the wind to help them scent-check does. The bucks' ability to determine the occupants' readiness by skirting the downwind side of a bedding area allows the hunter to effectively predict how most bucks will travel.

Setting stands 20 to 40 yards out from the downwind sides of doe-bedding areas is a good bet. However, when hunting large bedding areas, it's helpful to narrow movement down further. If a natural pinch point isn't present, the next best option is a stand placement that also covers the bedroom's main entrance and exit routes.

The final touch is a creative scent strategy: Because bucks are already cruising these bedding areas for does, estrus scents can be very effective at bringing them in for the shot. Estrus-drenched scent wicks can be placed on both sides of the stand to cut off bucks before they hit the hunter's odor stream. If a buck takes a route farther downwind than anticipated, he'll hit one of the two wicks' odor stream before encountering the hunter's scent.

Though one can never remove the element of luck from hunting the breeding phase, hunters certainly can stack the odds in their favor. Hunting funnels and doe-bedding areas are two ways of doing just that.

GEARING UP FOR LATE-SEASON SUCCESS

Once breeding winds down, bucks' priorities shift drastically. Regardless of whether we're talking northern or southern regions, the stresses of the rut commonly cause mature bucks to lose 25-30% of their body weight.

At this point, a buck's primary interest no longer lies in cementing his standing in the buck hierarchy or in finding receptive does. Certainly, he is still more than happy to take advantage of breeding opportunities, but his primary focus is on surviving winter.

With food sources now at a seasonal low point, deer concentrate at the best options still available. In farm country, a standing row crop can draw them from over 10 miles away. In the big woods, fresh new growth after logging can be a deer magnet. In northern regions, traditional yarding areas are capable of pulling deer from incredible distances. All of these activities are aimed toward increasing their odds of survival.

As in early season, finding Mr. Big and nailing his food source is critical. Furthermore, when the temps dip below the seasonal average for your hunting area, the same early-season stand-placement strategies can work well.

However, the key to that placement strategy working is most often the temperature. When the temps drop significantly below normal, as opposed to feeding during the late-night hours, deer have survival incentive to shift their feeding activities to the comparatively warmer late afternoon hours. When that occurs, the amount of daylight feeding can be significant.

Unfortunately, when temps are in the normal to warm range, many bucks hardly move during daylight. For that reason, the same tactics used during the lull phase must be implemented.

As a side note, hunting close to buck-bedding areas is the tactic of choice during any conditions that lead bucks toward more nocturnal activities. For those who struggle with finding bedding areas, techniques that remove much of the challenge will be covered in Chapter 9.

Regardless of which approach is used, one must understand that these deer are now more hypersensitive to disturbances than at any other point in season. They have survived the war of firearms and most of bow season by knowing the importance of avoiding humans.

That makes it even more critical to keep disturbances to a minimum and get it right the first time. If a stand is positioned on the wrong trail, the hunter gets winded or the access route in or out spooks deer, the chances of success go down dramatically. Even more than during any other phase of bow season, late-season hunters don't get many second chances.

With all that said, late season may be the best-kept secret of hunting. Many of my very best hunts have occurred under the most miserable conditions that late season can throw at a hunter.

During the second rut, decoys can be effectively used to pull bucks to your location. Though buck decoys are the author's choice during most of season, during the breeding and second-rut phases, he prefers to use either just a doe decoy or a buck-and-doe combination.

CAPITALIZING ON THE SECOND RUT

When it comes to the second rut, my entire strategy revolves around finding where the family groups are feeding. Find that and you will almost always find the bucks, regardless of the abundance or complete lack of buck sign. The second rut is very hit-and-miss. Unlike the first go around, the breeding window isn't nearly as tight and nowhere near as many females are available.

Frankly, the second rut can happen any day of late season and will most often occur in several little bursts. In most of the whitetail's upper Midwest and northern range, I believe that determining the second rut by adding 28 days to peak breeding is a myth. That date is when does that missed the first go around will come back into estrus. Though I don't dispute the estrous cycle, I simply don't believe that enough does are missed the first time they come into estrus to be a factor. Instead, I believe that fawns coming into estrus for the first time make up the majority of the second-rut breeding opportunities in these regions. Down south, I credit the late breeding of does to the breeding phase being spread out over a much longer period of time. In either case, I believe that predicting when these breeding opportunities will occur is impossible.

Though bucks rarely will go wandering in search of second-rut breeding opportunities, they certainly won't them pass up. Because there aren't many breeding opportunities left, we can use this to our advantage.

Mature bucks can still respond very positively to estrous scents. Often, because they aren't already with a doe, bucks will actually respond better than they did during the first rut. Because of that, it only makes sense to use strategically placed scent wicks to draw bucks to our stand. That's particularly beneficial when hunting stands that guard broader areas, such as food sources.

Estrous scents are even more effective when paired with doe decoys. With the exception of late season and the breeding phase, I most commonly use buck decoys. Not only do I believe they are more effective during most of season, but they also work to keep does away. Frankly, when does spend much time near a decoy, it almost always ends with a snorting-and-foot-stomping fest. However, during the breeding and second-rut phases, I feel decoys draw bucks much better when used as a doe.

Decoys work most effectively during late season when stands can't be placed in the thick of the action. Often, because of the sheer numbers of deer that prime late-season food sources draw, it can be impossible to place stands downwind of all the deer. In such cases, it's best to place stands in areas less desirable, but safer to hunt. The risk of does hanging around the decoy will be minimized. At the same time, the combination of a quality estrous scent, decoy and a few estrous calls can be just the ticket to drawing a buck across a food source.

As I'm sure you gathered from what I wrote earlier in this section, I don't really believe that you can separate the second rut from late season. To me, they both consist of the same time period, and which one is dominant on any given day will be decided by the doe-fawn's readiness.

Still, I break the late season and second rut into separate phases because of the hunting techniques used for both. As far as choosing which one to use on a given day, I begin hunting late-season strategies for the first few weeks after the breeding phase concludes. After that, I'll switch between late-season and second-rut strategies fairly regularly, allowing the weather to decide which I'll use most often. If it's nasty cold, I'm hunting the food sources. If it's mild, I'm back by the bed. To switch things up occasionally,

I'll pull out the scents and decoys. Of course, if I see breeding signs, I'll focus more heavily on second-rut strategies for a while. At the very least, routinely changing things keeps the deer off balance and the stands fresher.

CONCLUSION

With the number of changes that occur to the habitat and food sources, as well as those the bucks endure, it's no wonder that pitifully few stand locations are good from opening day to the close of season. Staying in bucks the entire season requires that stand sites be shifted to take advantage of what drives bucks during each phase. Doing that is the ticket to making hunting each phase of season as productive as it can be. ■

Spring is the best time to find hot scrapes to hunt during the upcoming season, but they can still be uncovered during season. However, one must be careful not to educate deer with careless scouting trips.

6. Secrets for Hunting the Hot Food Source

As I'm sure you noticed in the last chapter, food plays a vital role in both a buck's life and in our hunting strategies. Simply put, if you don't know what bucks are feeding on during the early and late phases of season, the odds of taking a good buck are slim.

Under certain conditions, hunting food sources can also be good during other phases of season—when hunting areas where pressure is low or virtually nonexistent, for example. More of these areas exist than many would first think.

Anyone who controls 500 or more acres of deer habitat in the Midwest has considerable ability to manage the amount of pressure deer there perceive. The same is true for large plantations and ranches in south Texas. Surprisingly, many of the larger, big-woods tracts of public land also have pockets of limited or nonexistent pressure. Hunter surveys in heavily hunted states, such as Wisconsin, Michigan and Pennsylvania, have all shown that hunting pressure drops dramatically even as little as half-a-mile off the road. In any of these settings, daylight feeding can consistently occur during any phase of season.

Even during the rut, food sources play a vital role in a mature buck's life. For one thing, contrary to what many hunters believe, bucks do continue to feed during the breeding phase. Granted, feeding may not be their top priority, but they still require nutrition to maintain the grueling pace they set for themselves.

Perhaps more importantly, feeding is always a high priority for does. Since bucks hunt does during the breeding phase, it's impossible to argue that identifying hot food sources isn't beneficial even while the breeding phase is in full swing.

Finally, outside of the chase and breeding phases, the majority of buck travels consist of transitioning between feeding and bedding in the mornings and bedding and feeding in the evenings. Sure, during the scrape phase, bucks will go out of their way to tend hot scrapes. Still, even then they are most often coming from the general direction of either their feeding or bedding areas. Even when you're hunting far away from the source, knowing what the deer are feeding on gives you the advantage of being able to more accurately predict a buck's direction of travel.

As you can see, identifying the hot food source of the moment is beneficial in many ways. Since it plays such a vital role in whitetails' lives, that only makes sense.

UNDERSTANDING THE SLIDING SCALE

The question then becomes, "What's Mr. Big's favorite food?" Frankly, the answer is ever changing, based largely on the combination of what's available, its growth state and its quality. For example, most know that the acorns from white oaks can be an extremely powerful draw for deer. However, that knowledge doesn't do much good when the conditions cause a mast crop failure; either the acorns are riddled with worms or they aren't mature when they fall. Either way, the deer won't be feeding heavily on them.

Looking at how deer feed on soybeans provides further insight. To begin with, soybeans are highly desired in their green state, when they are tender, easily digestible and high in protein. Because of that, deer devour the tops, leaves and even the green pods. However, once the beans brown, their desirability drops.

About the same time soybeans mature, acorns and other mast crops, such as apples and persimmons, are often hitting their ideal states. When this combination of events occurs, deer shift a significant portion of their feeding to the new and other previously existing options. Eventually, those options run out or mature past their peak.

In turn, the dried soybeans climb back up the desirability ladder. It's not because the beans have suddenly become better again; they have remained relatively constant. It's just that other foods disappeared or spoiled, and

In settings where numerous feeding options are available, being able to determine the hot food source of the moment is most critical to success.

Remote food sources where deer will feel safe, such as small, secluded fields and natural in-woods options, have the potential to receive more daylight feeding than large, open crop fields.

that narrowing of options moved the soybeans back toward the top of the deer's menu.

Then there is the fact that deer's nutritional needs change over the course of season. A protein-rich diet is still an important consideration during the early portion of fall to aid in antler development, milk production and body growth. Though both milk production and antler development are either done or reaching their end, growth and muscle development still occur during the early season. Therefore, during the early season, foods high in protein, such as alfalfa, clovers, soybeans and cool-season grass and weeds, are more highly sought.

Later, as the ever-shortening photoperiod signals deer to halt growth and build fat supplies, foods high in carbohydrates and/or fats, such as corn and acorns, become more important. High-carb, high-fat foods are even more important to mature bucks right before, during and immediately after the rut. This is due to the significant weight loss they endure during the breeding phase and the need to build back up for winter survival.

I'm certainly not implying that deer won't eat shelled corn in summer or a high-protein food source in winter, if available. They will. However, their nutritional needs are not the same throughout the year and their diet often changes to reflect that.

There are other factors to consider as well. For one, all else being equal, the food sources that provide relatively easy and safe access will experience heavier feeding than those that are difficult to get to or don't provide an illusion of safety.

It only stands to reason that the safer deer feel feeding in a location, the more likely daylight feeding will occur. Isolated clear-cuts, remote pockets of mountain laurel or Japanese honeysuckle, oak ridges deep within the timber or small fields or field fingers that are flanked by thick protective cover are all likely to experience heavier daylight feeding than a wide-open crop field.

The overall health and condition of the food crop also plays a role. All else being equal, a properly maintained and treated clover field will be selected over one that is growing in acidic, low-fertility soil, with plants that have been allowed to go to seed. Fresh, healthy acorns draw incredibly better than rotten or wormy options.

Finally, I believe that deer crave a diverse diet. I believe they get sick of eating the same thing every day. This was well illustrated when I used to feed wild deer during the late-winter months. The feed I supplied consisted of one-part corn with two-parts wheat and three-parts Antler King Pelleted Deer & Elk Feed. Frankly, it was impossible for deer to find a better, more nutritious food source in nature. Because of that, deer would flock to my feeding stations in winter by the hundreds.

However, as soon as spring melt began, the number of deer utilizing the feeding stations would immediately drop to single digits. Spring green up was still nearly a month away, so it wasn't like they suddenly had better options. I believe that they simply had grown so tired of eating the same thing each day, they preferred to eat dead grass. It taught me that deer crave diversity in their diet.

PUTTING IT ALL TOGETHER

I suspect that by now some readers are beginning to think that applying all of these factors to predict a hot food source is a bit overwhelming. After all, food sources that are hot one week can be ice-cold the next.

It's not only the growth stage of a food source that has an impact on its desirability; it's also the deer's changing nutritional needs. One must consider the health of the plants, how easy they are to get to and how safe deer feel feeding there. If all that weren't enough, deer will eat darn near everything, but they tire of eating the same thing all the time.

Though I firmly believe all of that's true, applying those factors really isn't as challenging as it may first appear.

For one, we can trim the list of preferred food sources to some of the most common and highly sought after. There are many foods that deer will eat, but they either don't occur in high enough concentrations or they are so low on the desirability list, they aren't worth our time.

For manageability's sake, I'll break the most highly sought-after foods into

Preseason glassing of hard-mast trees and the inspection of soft-mast producers helps to determine what trees will be producing this coming fall.

agricultural and native groupings. However, I must ask the readers to keep two things in mind: First, though I've tried to address the most common food sources of the north, south, east and west, this is certainly not an all-encompassing list. Regional differences will result in some prime feeding options not being present in certain areas, and some foods that are heavily used in one area not being listed. The other thing to keep in mind is that in farm country, native foods draw more feeding than most hunters give them credit for.

Beginning with cultivated crops, when still in their growing stage, soybeans and peas are tough to beat early in season. Alfalfa, clovers and hay, in that order, are also good bets at this time, particularly during or immediately after rainfall. However, if these plants are left to mature, burn out or experience repeated frosts, their desirability plummets and the amount of feeding activity they receive will directly depend on what other options are available. Of course, because of the temperature differences, in southern regions they can be great draws all season long.

As season progresses, matured and dried soybeans, sorghum and corn are very good choices. As we get even later, wheat, barley, rye, turnips and even potatoes can heat things up.

As native food sources go, it's tough to beat healthy white oak acorns whenever they are on the ground. The mast of red oaks comes in second to the whites, but unless the area sports an inexhaustible supply of white oak acorns, the acorns from red oaks will also get cleaned up. The same can be said of beech nuts and the pods of locust trees.

Persimmons, pears, apples and peaches I view as candy crops. When mature and available, deer will often feed heavily on them. Another candy crop are the leaves of sugar maples. When they first change color and begin falling, they are devoured by deer.

Speaking of leaves, the green leaves of many saplings associated with clear-cuts, such as poplar and aspen, as well as the leaves of vines and bushes like honeysuckle, mountain laurel and berries, are also fed on until they brown and die. Another great early-season choice can be found in meadows. Though they may appear dead, the cool season grasses and weeds in meadows are both high in protein and easily digestible.

Later in the season, feeding often shifts heavily to the tender shoots of woody browse. Though the twigs of virtually any conveniently placed deciduous tree will be nipped at some time, softwoods are most beneficial and more desired than hardwoods.

A general rule of thumb is that the smaller the tree or bush, the harder it will get hammered. When looking at evergreens, in general, the smaller and more tender the needles, the more they'll be eaten. Finally, northern white cedar is tough to beat. It's the only browse species known to be able to support a deer's life without requiring supplements from other browse species.

With a general list of prime food sources, late-summer months can be used to help narrow the field even further. Simply stopping in and asking the farmer when crops were planted and when he believes they will mature helps nail the timing issues. Additionally, inspecting the farm crops provides the opportunity to check their overall health. If a corner of the field is stunted or thriving, it will have a significant impact on where feeding will occur.

Keeping tabs on weather patterns can also be helpful. If the growing season is too wet or

Quizzing farmers on when they planted their crops, if they applied fertilizers equally to all, and when their anticipated harvest dates are, can be a big help in determining when each farm crop will be the most heavily sought after.

too dry, both farm and nature's crops will suffer. All else being equal, during years with harsh droughts, common sense says that potential food sources in low ground will draw better. The reverse is true for extremely wet years.

Getting out during late summer also provides the opportunity to gauge what the area's mast-crop production will be like. Many factors contribute to bountiful mast crops, mast-crop failure and points in-between. Inspecting how much fruit apple trees hold lets you know if they will provide much drawing power.

You can gauge acorn production the same way: Glass the oaks for developing acorns. If it appears that the mast crop will be poor, finding the few oaks that will produce good crops has put me in a surplus of deer many times. This inspection also avoids wasting time on an oak ridge that isn't yielding acorns.

A few other in-season tasks will further help keep us in the hot food source of the moment. Occasional mid-day scouts through known food sources, hidden within the woods, reveals where heavy feeding activity is occurring. Time spent on the stand can be productive as well. When a deer is sighted, being alert to what it may be feeding on provides added information.

Finally, sharing notes with your hunting buddies about what deer are currently feeding on can be very helpful. So is building a network of contacts with school bus drivers, milk haulers, farmers or county employees. They all spend time in deer country during feeding times. Their observations can be a huge help.

The combination of all these details is typically enough to keep up on feeding changes.

CONCLUSION

Though many factors are involved, being able to predict hot food sources can be broken down into manageable segments.

The first lies in understanding that few if any food sources will be good from the opener to the close. Next, one must figure out what prime food sources the area holds. After that, the job becomes identifying what state of maturity makes each most desirable, and narrowing down the likely window of time when they'll reach that state. At that point, we're well over halfway there.

Now comes the fine-tuning process: Summer inspection and weather patterns are helpful in determining what specific locations will be most heavily sought after. During season, low-impact scouting trips and the observations made by you and your network of friends will help assure that you stay on top of the flavor of the day.

Finally, when all else is equal, look for the food source that is both highly desired and most limited in supply. For example, when hunting a big-woods setting that's producing a bumper crop of acorns, the lone isolated meadow or clear-cut is a great choice.

Of course, the majority of feeding will be on the fallen fruit. However, you can bet that the deer will also want some greens. Because there's so much less of it available, chances of being in the right spot when Mr. Big decides he wants a salad are much greater than finding the one tree in the sea of oaks he decides to feed under any given day. Really, almost every aspect of nailing hot food sources involves playing the odds. ■

When you really boil it all down, consistently taking mature bucks like this is largely due to successfully addressing numerous seemingly minor details.

Since most of the scrapes that are being hit consistently back in the woods are done by nighttime visitors, even during the peak scraping phase, hunting scrapes too early in the season typically does nothing more than educate bucks to your presence.

When bucks work scrapes, it is very likely that their primary goals are to advertise their presence to all other deer and intimidate rival bucks.

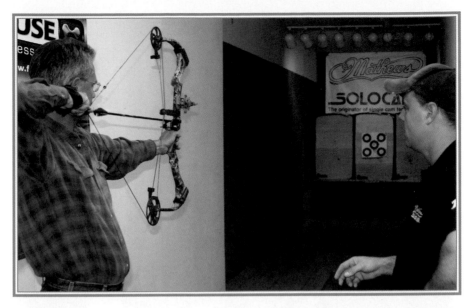

Traditional practice techniques are great for getting sighted-in, but do virtually nothing to prepare the hunter for making shots on deer.

Topo maps are excellent tools to help determine where deer travel on the land you hunt. They also allow you to "scout" from the comfort of your home.

Seeing this fresh rub was what caused Pat Reeve to further investigate the area and hang the stand from which he harvested his monstrous buck.

Adjusting the center shot is required when arrow groupings migrate left or right at various distances.

Setting stands in the backyard offers a chance to test them for unwanted noises before putting them to use in the deer woods.

Covering the area on the riser around the rest with felt or mole's skin fabric removes the risk of an arrow "tinking" against the riser at the wrong time.

A powdered wind detector helps you see the exact direction your scent is being carried. With wind currents and breezes changing throughout the day, using a product like this will help you plan your strategy more effectively.

By factoring in what wind directions would make the stand location the best, I was able to take this wide, high-beamed nine-point on the stand's first sit.

7. The Facts About Interpreting Deer Sign

During the predawn hours of November 14, Minnesota's Pat Reeve and his cameraman, Jim Musil, climbed into their stands to film another hunt for *Driven 24/7*. Being a veteran of capturing trophy buck hunts on film, memorable experiences are not rare for Pat. Little did he know that this day would turn out to be more memorable than any hunting experience he'd ever had before.

In reality, like many other hunts from stands, the hunt truly began while scouting. In this particular instance, it was almost scouting by accident. Pat had been to Schuyler County Illinois' Sugar Creek Outfitters scouting the previous spring. Based on those findings, he headed out with Sugar Creek's head guide, Chad John, on the rainy afternoon of November 12 to slap up stands for his hunt.

The true irony was that they were actually going out to hang another stand when Pat made a last-second decision about an unplanned addition. The combination of a little luck, a keen eye and his ability to interpret mature buck sign were the keys to his eventual encounter with a truly world-class buck.

The stand they'd intended to hunt was the tip of a cut on a thick side hill. The cut created pinch points on the top and bottom. Because of his findings in the spring, they were headed for the top.

"As we drove ATVs in," recalled Pat, "we passed right by the funnel at the bottom and could see thigh-size rubs. Arriving up top, Chad told me that he'd been in there a little while ago and those rubs weren't there. So, after hanging the stand up top, we went down to take a closer look. I'm glad we did. Not only were the fresh rubs encouraging, but the trails were much more impressive than they appeared in spring."

Jumping forward to November 14, the morning's slow start changed fast when a doe came running in, dragging a buck behind her. With a tree blocking Pat's view, the only reason he knew it was a shooter was because of an excited whisper from his cameraman.

"When the deer finally got to where I could see it," Reeve said, "my first thought was, 'Oh my Gosh. It's a Booner!' He was still about 60 yards away in brush, walking toward us."

After some anxious moments, it all came together. "When he hit my wider 20-yard shooting lane," Pat recalled, "I voice-grunted to stop him. After getting the OK from Jim, I took another second to be sure my 20-yard

Pat Reeve and cameraman Jim Musil pose with the huge buck that resulted from Pat's ability to read fresh buck sign.

pin was on him and let the arrow fly. I knew before I hit him that it was a good shot."

The sweeping beamed, high-tined 10-point turned out to be considerably bigger than Reeve first believed. Even after the drying period, the buck came in as a 203-inch gross typical. Though learning to interpret buck sign doesn't guarantee those types of results, Pat Reeve would be the first to affirm that it played a critical role in his arrowing that buck. Frankly, it plays a critical role in taking many other mature bucks, as well.

Mature bucks are a different species of deer. In most areas, because of the intense hunting pressure they endure, they place a higher premium on safety than other deer must, or they die. Because of that, during most of deer season, they are loners. They most often have different bedding areas, utilize different trail systems and may even sacrifice prime food sources for lesser quality, safer options.

Furthermore, they tend to be more temperamental than other deer. Because they have learned to survive by avoiding daylight encounters with hunters, it often doesn't take as much of a push for them to change their patterns as it does with other deer.

Because of their loner tendencies and propensity to alter their patterns, the ability to read mature buck sign becomes critical to achieving consistent success for much of the season. This is so true that, during all but the chase, breeding and second-rut phases, I'd always much rather set up on a relatively small quantity of fresh, quality big-buck sign than on massive quantities of pure deer sign. To differentiate quality from quantity, the ability to interpret mature buck sign is required.

READING RUBS

Because most hunters consider rubs the most accurate form of sign for identifying big bucks, let's begin with them. When it comes to reading sign, I've always found that finding it isn't enough. If hunters truly are to interpret sign and use it to their advantage, they must be able to formulate an educated guess as to how it fits in the big picture and if the creator is likely to pass the area again during daylight. To accomplish that, one must understand why the sign was left to begin with—the buck's purpose for making the rub.

Though some early rubs certainly are due to the velvet-shedding process, they are in the minority, and it has been my experience that the few made during velvet shedding aren't nearly as impressive as those made after. Velvet-shedding rubs most often involve the use of branches or small saplings. When one considers that their purpose is to remove velvet, not to

Clusters of rubs back off from open food sources identify staging areas. When the rubs indicate a mature buck's activities, this can be a great spot to set up for afternoon hunts.

stand out as signposts to other deer or to vent aggression, it only makes sense that they often aren't anywhere near as visually obvious as later rubs. It simply isn't their function.

Primarily, non-velvet shedding rubs, referred to strictly as rubs from this point forward, serve as communication tools. Research has strongly indicated that they convey both visual and olfactory messages to other whitetails. In essence, rubs are a means of advertising an individual buck's presence, providing a general indication of his maturity and serving to intimidate other bucks.

Furthermore, the act of rubbing provides an avenue for building the strong neck muscles required for fighting and venting frustrations. As the rut grows closer and testosterone levels rise, a mature buck becomes much like a bomb ready to explode. Something as innocent as hearing another buck grunt in the distance can inspire a mature buck to thrash a tree. Along

with venting frustrations and building muscles, this act also displays power to possible observers. That display has the potential to further intimidate a pro-spective combatant into submission.

As it applies to using rubs to gauge the maturity of the maker, almost every serious hunter knows to get excited when they find a shredded tree with the diameter of a man's thigh. The myth is that immature bucks won't also rub large trees. They do. The dif-ference becomes apparent in the amount of damage they can achieve.

As with immature bucks, the big boys also hit many smaller-diameter trees, saplings and brush. This is particularly true of early-season rubs, when

Because younger bucks will occasionally rub large trees, both the height of the rub and width of the tine gouges can be used to determine a buck's relative maturity on large trees with little rub damage.

When the shiny sides of trees in a rub line either consistently point toward the feeding or bedding area, rub lines can reveal the buck's travel direction and indicate if the travel corridor would be better suited for morning or afternoon hunts.

testosterone levels and aggression are both comparatively low. The majority of early-season rubs appear on unimpressive trees.

The key to gauging the maturity of the makers of rubs really lies in the damage done to the tree. During inspection, simply ask yourself if you believe a young buck would do this level of damage to the object. More often than not, the reduced power and testosterone levels result in young bucks creating nothing more than a small bare strip on saplings or two narrowly spaced, relatively low gouges from their bow tines on larger trees.

Conversely, a mature buck's increased bulk and nasty temperament is bad news for saplings. Long peals, twisted branches and snapped trees get me every bit as excited as calf-sized rubs. When it comes to larger trees, the big boys often shred them. Even when they don't explode on the tree in a fit of aggression, the height of the rub and spacing of the tines typically give the maker's size away.

Frankly, the young bucks rarely do much damage and, although mature bucks will sometimes also rub low, their rubs are almost always low. That is due to the increased need to use leverage to their advantage. When using rubs to gauge the maker's maturity, all of these factors must be considered. Of course, if the rub is fresh, it never hurts to check for track size either.

Yet another difference between mature and immature bucks' rubbing tendencies can be seen. In a nutshell, young bucks make far fewer rubs and begin rubbing in earnest much closer to the breeding phase due to their relative inexperience and slower-rising testosterone levels. The combination works to retard the 1.5- and 2.5-year-old bucks' signposting endeavors, so a collection of early rubs typically indicates the presence of a mature buck.

As discussed previously, before the chase phase occurs, most buck travels consist of transitioning between bedding, food and water. Therefore, it stands to reason that most rubs occur around food and water sources, bedding areas and the trails connecting the three.

Ultimately, rub lines are nothing more than a series of otherwise unrelated rubs that a buck makes over numerous trips between these three destinations. In general, the more trees suitable for rubbing that exist along the travel corridors and the more often the buck takes the route, the more defined the rub lines become.

Not only do rub lines indicate buck travel corridors, they can also provide insight into the buck's direction of travel. That is determined by studying the side of the tree that's rubbed; that's the side the buck was coming from.

This can be useful when determining whether a stand placed along a buck's travel corridor is best for hunting mornings, afternoons or both.

Take a well-established rub line connecting a bedding area to a clear-cut, for example. If the majority of rubbed sides of the trees face toward the bedding area, chances are good that they were made over the course of numerous evening trips to the food source, as the buck transitioned from bedding to feeding. Conversely, if the shined sides are on the clear-cut side, they were most likely made when the buck returned to bed in the morning. Finally, a somewhat equal mix indicates that he uses the same trail both going to and returning from feeding.

As useful as this can be, basing decisions on one or two rubs can lead to incorrect assumptions. Rubs are made as a buck walks along. When the tree lies in his path, he'll most often trash it from the direction he was approaching, providing an accurate guide to where he was coming from.

However, if it lies off his path, the angle he takes to reach it can create misleading results. Furthermore, I've occasionally witnessed bucks circle a tree before rubbing. And if a tree has an angle to it or large branches that make access to part difficult, the buck commonly adjusts his stance to provide the best access to the portion of the tree most easily rubbed.

It's best to only use rub lines to predict travel direction when the majority of rubs tell the same story. By refraining from making assumptions based on one or two rubs, as well as factoring in the possible need to veer off course and access issues, rub lines can be very accurate indicators of travel direction.

Along with travel corridors, food and water sources and bedding areas, concentrations of rubs can also reveal staging areas. A survival mechanism that mature bucks often use is to hang back from open food sources, such as agricultural fields, clear-cuts and meadows. They will burn time in these staging areas until either darkness arrives or enough other deer expose themselves to this potentially dangerous open area to assure the buck of its safety. When burning time, bucks often mark these staging areas with rubs.

Because of that, when a concentration of rubs are found, commonly twenty to one hundred yards off the edge of an open food source, it's a good bet that it identifies the location as a staging area. When the rubs show that a good buck is burning time here, this can be a great location to pick up his early evening movements. Often, encounters during legal shooting hours can occur in staging areas with bucks that won't step foot into feeding areas until after dark. Clusters of rubs can be used to identify these valuable stand locations.

UNDERSTANDING SCRAPES

Scrapes are yet another valuable bit of sign which hunters must be able to accurately interpret. These large, bowled-out, pawed areas of dirt scream bucks so loudly that few hunters can refrain from getting excited at the sight

When bucks work scrapes, it is very likely that their primary goals are to advertise their presence to all other deer and intimidate rival bucks.

of them. What many don't realize is the sort of complex messages these signposts relay and the effects they have on other deer.

For years, scrapes were thought of as really nothing more than pickup bars designed for and by bucks. Many researchers speculated that a buck made scrapes to attract estrous does for breeding. Although that happens on occasion, many years and countless hours of research later, the popular belief amongst scientists is changing. More and more, studies are indicating that scrapes are utilized to a greater extent as intricate communication and intimidation tools, rather than as meat markets.

In many ways, scrapes are not unlike the whitetail world's version of a billboard. They are an elaborate combination of advertising and information. It is theorized that scrapes communicate a buck's dominance, identity and other information of social importance. It is believed that bucks deposit odor-based messages that convey such information, having physiological and psychological impact upon other deer.

Breaking down a scrape into components can help illustrate how they may be able to provide all this information. Most hunters realize that any serious, hard-hit scrape has a licking branch hovering above it that is repeatedly worked by bucks. This is a key component of the site. They lick it, chew it, rub their foreheads on it and even thrash it about with their antlers. In the process, it is believed that they deposit chemical signals that advertise their presence, as well as their individual identity.

Along with working the licking branch, they also typically paw the ground to create the traditional oval shape that many think of as the scrape itself. Until someone actually holds a conversation with a deer, it is impossible to tell exactly why. However, the theory that this act displays aggression and a willingness to fight to prove dominance does make sense. I also believe that it also has a degree of visual appeal to possibly attract deer from upwind.

Finally, we have the act of urinating on the scrape. Early in fall, deer typically do this without involving their tarsal glands. Later, during the peak scraping phase, bucks perform the act of rub urinating by pinching their back knees together to draw their tarsal glands close and dribbling their urine over them, ultimately depositing it on the scrape. From these odors, it's believed that other deer can decipher the social and physiological status of the maker, which may inform them of such things as the buck's dominance, health and readiness to breed. To further support this, it has been found that the compounds in a buck's urine that relate to age and dominance only appear during the peak scraping, chase and breeding phases of season.

Over the years, I've read and heard other "experts" break scrapes into classes such as breeding, territorial, boundary, core area and about 50 other groups. To this, I say hogwash. Frankly, I don't buy for a second that bucks purposefully travel the edges of their home range and make scrapes to serve as territory markers. Do I believe they make some scrapes near the edges of their home range? Sure. As stated in an earlier chapter, a mature buck can make over 200 scrapes in a single season. Some are bound to occur along the edges of his home range, as well as in his core area. However, I don't buy that a buck is capable of consciously thinking, "I'm going to create a scrape here for breeding, one there to mark my core area, yet another to show this is my territory and then finish up with a lap of scrapes around the boundary of my home range."

This isn't meant to say that bucks' scrapes can't be grouped into classifications. I believe they can. Essentially, I break them into three groupings: scrapes they'll likely never revisit, scrapes they work fairly regularly, and individual scrapes that numerous bucks all work together.

Because mature bucks can make so many scrapes, it stands to reason that most are spur-of-the-moment, random scrapes. Most likely because they aren't placed where the buck passes often, they're created and forgotten. I also include the scrapes made by immature bucks in this group because, frankly, they have no clue what they're really doing. They have urges and see the cool big guys making scrapes. So they become copycats, really not having the maturity or experience to understand the purpose behind their actions.

Next, there are the scrapes that occur along an individual buck's travel corridor. Because he routinely uses the trail connecting his bedding and feeding areas, "transitioning" from one area to another, he also routinely freshens one or more scrapes he's made along that path. When he's in the right frame of mind and a licking branch is staring him in the face, I don't believe he can help but make or refresh a scrape. If the maker of this kind of scrape is a good buck, such transitional scrapes can be great to hunt.

Lastly, there are primary scrapes—those that occur in specific locations that concentrate high numbers of deer. It may be in the back corner of an alfalfa field, the intersection of two heavily used logging roads, the downwind side of a doe-bedding area or anywhere else that numerous deer frequent. In each case, many deer pass a specific location and it serves as an effective spot to place a billboard for advertising. Young and old bucks alike hit it again and again, most often year after year. When positioned in areas where bucks feel safe, these can also be very exciting places to hunt.

As covered in Chapter 5, spring is the best time to locate scrapes for hunting—the time when one can truly evaluate their level of use. After tossing out the ones that weren't used much, one can determine whether the scrape occurs along a specific buck's travel corridor or in a high-use area. From that, you can determine whether it falls within the transitional or primary scrape slot. Then, it's simply a matter of figuring out if the area makes sense to hunt.

Making these determinations on scrapes found during season is a little trickier. When a new found scrape is first opened up, I know of no way to consistently determine whether it will become a heavily utilized scrape or not. I simply rely on the amount of mature buck sign in the area and woodsmanship to decide if it's worthy of hunting.

Finding scrapes that have been open for a while makes the job easier. If the chase phase is still a ways off and the scrape is in an area likely to observe daylight activity, seeing large tracks in the scrape is all I need to give the spot a chance.

READING TRACKS

Speaking of deer tracks, I believe they are often the most-overlooked piece of deer sign left in the woods. How many times do hunters push aside a few leaves to study a trail in detail, looking for large tracks to verify that a mature buck is using it?

A fairly obvious and general, but pretty darn accurate, statement is that big bucks have big tracks. Knowing this can be applied to scouting in several ways. First, because family groups and mature bucks commonly use different trails, finding a mixture of adult and fawn tracks on that cow path of a trail running through the mature section of the woods allows us to easily identify it as a family group trail. When further examination reveals the absence of disproportionately large tracks, it's best to find a different location to hang a buck stand.

On the flip side, extra-large tracks on trails, in scrapes, around rubs, at water holes and anywhere else tracks can be found are a strong indicator of the presence of a mature buck. The benefits of finding these tracks are obvious.

When it comes to track size, I'm sure you noticed that I refrained from giving measurements. The reason for this is that the average size of a big buck track varies from area to area, particularly from north to south. A general rule of thumb is that the farther north you travel, the larger the subspecies of deer. This is because of the survival advantages of possessing a larger body in colder regions—the larger the body, the less energy is required to heat one body unit—and of having a smaller body in the hotter southern regions, making it easier to shed excess body heat. Heck, in Wisconsin alone, body sizes are noticeably smaller in the southern portions of the state than in the northern regions.

Because of that, providing track measurements would be doing most

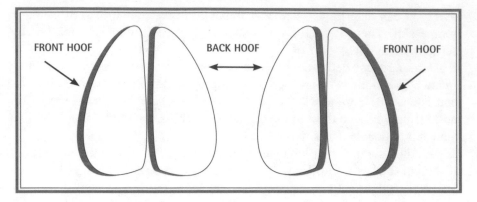

Because bucks have comparatively broader shoulders and narrower hips than does, their back hoof overlaps their front with an inside offset during a relaxed walk.

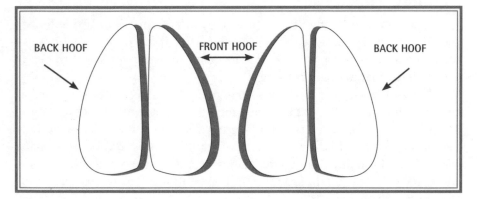

Because does have comparatively broader hips and narrower shoulders than bucks, their back hoof overlaps their front with an outside offset during a relaxed walk.

readers an injustice. About the best gauge I can offer is that a mature buck track is commonly 15-30% larger than that of a mature doe. Using that as a guide, most readers should be able to differentiate tracks. But remember that this is a generalization, and exceptions do occur.

As far as the rest of the popular methods of differentiating buck from doe tracks, I've never found them to be reliable. Dewclaws are evident in buck, doe and even fawn tracks when conditions are right. I've run across numerous does that dragged their hooves and just as many mature bucks that didn't.

However, along with size, there is another trait that can be used to consistently differentiate buck and doe tracks. Because of the advantages it provides for birthing fawns, does typically have wider hips. When walking naturally, the back hoof print overlaps the front track as wider hips cause the back track to overlap the front with an offset to the outside.

Much like men having smaller hips and wider shoulders than women, bucks also typically have wider shoulders than hips. That causes their back track to overlap their front with an inside offset. Knowing this enables one to study the tracks of walking deer and gauge their sex. When combined with track size, one can now use tracks to identify mature bucks.

CLUES PROVIDED BY SCAT

As with the myths associated with track size, I've never found any consistency to the old wives tale that bucks defecate in individual pellets, whereas doe scat is clumped. From my experiences, the clumped verses pelleted scat is due to what the deer has eaten and has nothing to do with its sex.

However, as a general rule of thumb, I have found that big bucks leave big piles of scat. As with everything, there are exceptions. Still, the more indicators that point toward the presence of a mature buck, the more it is likely to be a big guy.

One of the better values of deer droppings is the indication of feeding areas. When leaves around oaks are pawed and the area yields numerous piles of deer droppings, you can bet deer have been feeding there on acorns. Surpluses of scat in any potential food source show a high level of feeding.

Droppings also indicate if a food source is currently hot or already passed over. If all the droppings are old, chances are that the deer have moved to greener pastures. In turn, if there are either fresh piles intermixed with old, or exclusively fresh scat, you know that feeding is occurring now.

MAKING THE BED

As with tracks and scat, one can use certain guidelines to differentiate buck beds from family group bedding areas. As previously mentioned, bucks typically bed by themselves. Therefore, when various sized depressions are found in the leaves it's a pretty safe bet that it reveals a family group bedding area.

On the flip side, when a lone, large depression or a handful of similarly sized large depressions are found, it indicates a buck's bedroom. Though finding several beds can lead one to believe numerous animals are bedding there, the thing to key on is whether they're all large. Many times a buck will lay up in the same area, but not the same bed each time. If all the beds in an area are big, there's a good chance it's the work of a single buck.

When snow is on the ground, urine spots can be another indicator. Often, deer will urinate as soon as they rise from their beds. Because of differences in anatomy, a doe's urine spot is often at the edge of the bed, whereas the buck's urine spot tends to be in the center.

That alone is not enough to base an educated decision on; that's where adding more pieces to the puzzle comes into play. For example, it's a good bet that it's the bed of a good buck if the urine spot is in the center of a bed with large tracks leading away and no small beds are present. The addition of other big-buck indicators is what makes this a reliable trait.

CONCLUSION

Interpreting deer sign is more of an art than an exact science. When you really boil it down, it amounts to understanding sign and piecing as many bits of evidence together as one can. The more pieces one can put together, the more accurate the conclusions become. With that, we can make educated decisions on what's going on and where our odds are the highest of having a daylight encounter with Mr. Big. ■

Any location where deer tracks are left provides the opportunity to check for big-buck tracks. Overlooking this bit of sign is a huge mistake.

8. Following the Map to Trophy Bucks

S tudying the topographical-contour (or "topo") map, I knew I'd found a killer stand site. A sharp erosion cut sliced up the side of a steep wooded ridge, stopping about 20 yards short of a deep saddle. It was the merging of three funnel features into one. If the cut was even half as deep or the sides anywhere near as steep as the map indicated, deer would not want to cross it. They also wouldn't want to needlessly climb the extra 50-some feet of steep ridge that flanked both sides of the saddle. With the ridge snaking through the woods for over a mile, it was a safe bet that bucks would be running that as well. As if to add a cherry on top, the map showed that swampland, highly likely to be used as bedding areas, was positioned on both sides of the ridge. There was little doubt that this spot had tremendous potential.

Over a mile and a half from the nearest access point, with map in hand and a stand and set of climbing sticks on my back, I began the walk to see this funnel for myself. Though I'd only have one day I could hunt the spot, I was far from disappointed that I'd have to work this hard to get to the location. Because I was hunting public lands, I wagered the extra work of packing the stand in with me that the local hunters hadn't studied a topo map of the area, and that they'd be hunting much closer to the road. I was right, and I wasn't disappointed with what I'd found.

With the stand set, I made my way back to the funnel well before first light the next morning. Even as I climbed into the tree, I could hear the distinct trotting sounds of an approaching buck. Still well before first light, the large shadowy figure slipped through the saddle within easy bow range of my stand. I won't even pretend to know how big he was, but I can safely say he had a lot of bone on his head.

The rest of the day was one I'll cherish for the rest of my bowhunting days. From my stand, I can't even tell you how many different bucks I saw. As I put in my hunting logs, "somewhere between 12 and 17 different bucks, 2 or 3 of them shooters. Too many to give antler and age stats. The times ranged from before first light to 10 minutes before dark, with spurts of action spread out over the entire sit. They were everywhere, but more passed the stand than anything else. Only change would be to shift to the tree 10 yards down from southeast corner of saddle to pick up shots at where the two slob bucks crossed the cut. Amazing stand location! 9.5 (out of 10 rating)."

As you probably figured out, I didn't shoot a buck that day. I didn't even draw my bow. To be honest, the only reason I didn't was because I ignored some faint sign that occurred in a spot that was comparatively easier to cross than the rest of the cut. One big boy followed the cut up to that point and crossed there, instead of climbing the extra 20 yards to the tip. He may have been the same buck I'd seen before first light. The other was running the ridge side and crossed there. Still, although the property was being hunted heavily, the ability to effectively read topo maps had provided me with one of the best days I've ever had on a stand. If I hadn't had to leave the next day, who knows what it would have produced.

BENEFITS OF MAP READING

As was the case with that hunt, topo maps can be very valuable scouting tools. I personally rely on them so heavily, and have had such success using them to locate potentially hot stand locations, that I feel blind scouting without one.

One of the main benefits of reading topo maps comes from minimizing the risks of missing good stand sites. As the public-land hunters illustrated by missing the funnel stand setup that began this piece, while foot scouting it can be easy to miss stand sites that stick out like sore thumbs on a topo map. The bird's-eye view they provide displays a big picture that can't be seen from the ground.

Spending some time studying topo maps before you go afield can help you determine the best stand-placement sites, and how to reach them.

As beneficial as using maps to uncover stands may be during off-season scouting, it is even more so when in-season scouting is required. When scouting during the season, finding quality stands is certainly a goal. However, keeping deer ignorant of the fact that they're being hunted and not pushing them off their current patterns is every bit as important.

That's where the ability to read topo maps can be worth its weight in gold. Instead of blindly stumbling around the woods, if there is any relief to the property at all, one can find many of the most promising stand-site locations before even hitting the woods.

Of course, one still must foot scout the locations to gauge their true value. However, if you first generate a list of the top-potential spots, the lowest-impact routes to those locations can be determined. The ability to slip in and out, without trashing the entire woods scouting, greatly reduces the disturbances typically required to find a property's hot spots.

Another advantage that topo maps commonly provide is the ability to piece travel patterns together more effectively. Assuming a basic knowledge of the property's food sources, the topography often shows the best routes to and from these areas. Furthermore, many bedding sites are also based on topography. From simply knowing where the deer feed, the ability to read maps often enables savvy hunters to make educated guesses on where the deer bed and how they travel back and forth to feed.

Luckily, all of this can be accomplished through some basic map-reading skills and a little experience. Even for map-reading novices, learning to read topo maps can be relatively easy.

MAP READING 101

The United States Geological Survey's (USGS) 7.5-minute quadrangles (quads) are the basis for most topo maps. The USGS has quad coverage for all of the United States. Luckily, in today's computer age, there are several sources that offer printable versions for free, as well as numerous companies offering maps for sale. Because of USGS quads being so widely used, I'll use them as the standard for our exploration into map reading.

Let's begin by exploring cultural features, such as roads, railroad tracks, buildings and major transmission lines. USGS quads illustrate cultural features in black. This information alone can help set the stage for how you can gain access to areas and even suggest possible routes to stand sites.

Next, we have the wooded areas that are shaded in green. Aside from that obviously showing us where the woods are, narrowed-down necks of green can show potential funnels.

The hydrological features, such as swamps, rivers, lakes and ponds, also can show funnels. The narrow piece of dry land between those bodies

Topo maps have the potential to reveal excellent, low-impact routes for accessing a property and stands.

of water could be a good example of that. Rivers and streams often are used as travel corridors for deer, and they can serve as excellent low-impact routes to stands. A swamp is a potential bedding area. Finally, any hydrological feature can create barriers that many other hunters may avoid.

For whatever reason, many hunters are unwilling to put on a pair of waders or jump in a canoe to go deer hunting. This often results in mini-sanctuaries existing within areas that are heavily hunted. Studying a map can show you where these areas exist.

As helpful as the bird's-eye view of those features can be, showing the land in relief is often the greatest advantage contour maps provide. Each contour line on a map indicates a line of equal elevation, with a standard contour interval of 10 feet on most quads. That means if the 1250-foot contour is running along the side of a hill, the next contour going up the hill will represent the 1260-foot line, whereas the one going downhill would be the 1240. Although this does show us how far above sea level things are, the real purpose for hunters lies in showing relief.

Because they are lines of constant elevation and are at set intervals, contour lines show how relatively flat or steep the terrain is. When the contours are spaced relatively far apart, the terrain is fairly flat. Conversely, the closer they are together, the steeper the terrain. With this understanding, we can begin to see topographical features emerge.

One of the most basic features is a ridge. With contour lines on both sides stacked close together, increasing in elevation as they reach the top, a ridge is easily identifiable. In wooded areas, ridges often serve as natural travel corridors for deer. Typically, the family groups will have a worn trail on top, with fainter trails just off the sides that are used by bucks. During the rut, it is not uncommon for bucks to run ridge systems for miles while searching out hot does.

When a major ridge splits, the point before it breaks into two is also a good location. Because bucks are likely running the ridge hard, this point is almost like the intersection of two highways. When set up right, a hunter can cover the bucks running all three portions of the ridges, as well as those switching from one to another.

When the contours bulge out to the side of the ridge, it indicates a knob. When small, minor ridges shoot off the side, they show points. Wooded knobs and points are often used as bedding areas. Bucks tend to select the ones that allow them to use their eyes to see the lowland below and the wind to cover their backside. That combination provides bucks with the ultimate in safety.

Ridges pair with other features to create many different topographical funnels. For example, a saddle is nothing more than a dip in a ridge top. If you were to look at the profile of a saddle, you would see the top of the ridge runs fairly horizontally. Then, at some point, the ridge top would dip downward, only to rise back up and continue at its former elevation. It can be thought of almost like something has taken a huge bite out of the top of the ridge. The bottom of the dip is called the saddle.

When we find a location where the contour lines running along the top of the ridge wrap around to its opposite side, as if the ridge came to a tapering end, only to have the contours start up again, we have a saddle. On the map, it resembles two ridge tops in the process of converging and melting into one. As a side note, both the tapering end of a ridge and the high sides of saddles are potential bedding sites.

Because a saddle is lower than the ridge top on either side, deer often cross the ridge in the saddle. Simply put, they are lazy and don't want to expend extra energy unless there's a good reason to.

Another good topographical funnel are dry washes (cuts) running down the side of the ridge—cuts caused by erosion from years of focused runoff.

Once they erode to a certain point, they become difficult for deer to cross. To avoid doing so, many deer will either go up the ridge to cross at the upper tip of the cut or down the ridge to cross at the bottom.

When these cuts are deep enough to discourage crossing and go far enough up the ridge, they can be great stand sites. Sitting above the top of a cut can enable you to cover the traffic around the tip, along with the buck trail common to the upper edge of the ridge and the family group's ridgetop trail. The bottom of the cut, where the runoff begins fanning and the cut dissipates, can also produce good stand sites.

A cut is easily identified on a quad map by the contours V-ing into the side of the ridge, as they go up the side. In general, the narrower and more pronounced the V is, the sharper and steeper the sides of the cut are. Conversely, the more the series of contours each resemble a U, the more tapered the cut. These cuts are still worth investigating, however, and are often sharper than the map reveals.

Topo maps provide hunters with the ability to more effectively conduct in-season scouting on new properties while keeping disturbances to a minimum.

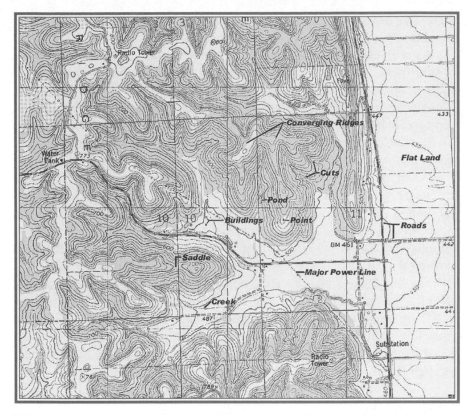

This topo map has two roads, two buildings, a power line, a pond, a creek, a point, two converging ridges, two cuts, a saddle and flatlands that are labeled. Study these features and find other examples on the map.

Another potentially good stand site is where several cuts come together near the bottom of the hill or ridge sides. Because deer tend to follow these cuts up and down, the convergence of cuts can create a busy intersection of deer trails. Stands placed along the side hills, above where the cuts converge, are good bets. But because swirling winds are the rule in these locations, only those who take odor control very seriously should attempt to hunt them.

A bench, yet another type of funnel, can be one of the best stands for rutting bucks there is. In a nutshell, a bench is a fairly flat strip of ground that runs along the side of a ridge, somewhere around halfway up.

It is common in ridge country to have farm crops planted in valleys that are flanked by wooded ridges on either side. In such a setting, the deer often bed high and feed low. Under these conditions, when a bench runs along the side of a ridge, a buck can scent-check the trail of every doe that's recently transitioned between feeding and bedding. Because of that, and because these flat areas offer easier walking than the steep sides of the ridge, benches often become highways for cruising bucks.

As with every other topographical feature, a bench will show up on a contour map. When looking at the stacked contours along the side of the ridge, keep an eye peeled for a gap somewhere around halfway up the ridge. Remember, tightly stacked contours show steep raises in elevation. When a gap appears between contours that are tightly stacked above and below it, you have a bench. Furthermore, the longer it snakes its way along the side of the ridge, the more productive the bench will likely be.

When it comes to funnels involving ridges, many of the very best are where two of these features converge. As was the case with the stand location at the beginning of this chapter, a good example is when a sharp cut begins near the base of a saddle. Here, the hunter can intercept bucks running the top of the ridge, those crossing at the saddle and the ones skirting the cut.

Flatland hunters also have the potential to find topographical funnels. Deer like to maintain low profiles; it increases their life expectancy. So they will commonly travel any dips or gullies that keep them hidden. Finding these low-profile areas on contour maps can identify places that deer use as travel routes. Look for areas where contour maps make "U"s as they meander through flatter areas.

CONCLUSION

As you can see, having the ability to read topo maps can provide tremendous advantages in finding stand sites, as well as keeping scouting and hunting impact at a minimum. The more one studies these maps, the better they become as more potential stand sites emerge.

To help build these skills, simply print out a topo map of your hunting land and put it to use during an off-season scout. When you come across topographical features, find them on the map and note how the contours appear. After no time at all, the features will begin making sense. Trust me, if you get nothing else from this book, the minimal effort it takes to learn how to read topo maps will pay for itself countless times over. ■

9. Insider Tips to Patterning Bucks

L arry Kline first saw the buck that would take him on a three-year quest while shining deer, a legal activity in Wisconsin. Right then and there, he decided that he wanted that animal. Later, after a scouting camera captured an eerily foggy picture of the buck, he became known to Larry's family and friends as the Ghost Buck. The buck's ability to vanish for long periods of time made the name fit even better yet.

"My dad had been telling some of our friends that I was obsessed with taking this buck," Larry told me. "The truth is that I was. The Ghost Buck had become a part of my entire family's life, and I wanted him bad. I was obsessed, but I viewed it as a healthy obsession."

Patterning the Ghost Buck took Larry Kline on a three-year quest before it finally ended in success.

Because of the big-woods setting the Ghost Buck lived in, sightings for Larry were rare. Instead, he had to focus on determining food sources, reading sign and making educated guesses. In his three years of hunting this magnificent animal, he had passed up many Pope & Young-class bucks, and he'd yet to see the Ghost Buck a single time from stand!

Then Larry got the break he needed. Checking his scouting camera on a morning before the season opened, he saw that he'd captured the Ghost Buck's photo. He intently studied the image of his property, doing his best to correlate the location shown with an idea about how the buck was using the ground. The more he studied the photo, the more convinced Larry became that the big deer was using a strip of jack pine that separated two of his food plots.

It made sense that the buck was using the strip for cover as he traveled to his bedding site after a night of feeding. Larry hoped to encounter the magnificent animal using the stand at the narrow point of that strip.

Opening morning found him perched in that stand. As he peered through the jack pines, he caught the movement of a large-bodied deer approaching. When it raised its head, Larry almost couldn't believe his eyes. There, working its way toward him, was The Ghost Buck. Several minutes and many frazzled nerves latter, the hunter put a killing shot on the local legend.

If I had a nickel for how many times I've heard "experts" talk about patterning bucks, I'd be a rich man. Whether it's in print, on TV or in seminars, the term is knocked around more than a tennis ball at Wimbledon. Ironically, for all the talk, they rarely ever say anything.

When you think about it, it makes sense that most experts have little of value to contribute. Frankly, patterning bucks takes time and effort. When TV personalities are expected to produce piles of antlers each season, most simply can't afford to invest the resources it takes to pattern one or more bucks. To a certain extent, publication deadlines impose the same constraints on many writers. I'm not saying that some experts don't actually pattern bucks. But I have no doubt that far more of them toss the term around simply to make themselves appear to be better hunters.

Patterning bucks takes work, woodsmanship, dedication and time. Even then, you are bound to strike out on far more bucks than you'll smash homers on. Still, it can be done. Furthermore, it's made far more doable if you understand the tricks of the trade.

OBSERVATIONS

The first step toward patterning a buck is identifying him. Certainly, large rubs, tracks and beds can all indicate that a mature animal is present, and there's absolutely nothing wrong with setting up on sign alone. However, if a hunter is going to dedicate the time and effort to a specific buck, he wants to see what he's after.

You might get the initial view of the buck in many different ways. Perhaps it is a distant sighting while you're hunting—a buck you kick up while walking to the stand—or a chance sighting while you're driving home from work. For those purposefully striving to find bucks to pattern, investing some morning and evening hours, slowly cruising back roads or past known food sources, is a common practice.

Another method is setting up to perform long-range observations of specific areas. For some reason, many seem to believe that such observations are exclusively for hunting food sources and farm country, and that there's

Treating long-range observations with the same respect you'd treat a hunt, such as paying attention to wind direcion, helps ensure that these activities go undetected by the bucks you're trying to pattern.

no benefit for big-woods hunters. That's simply not true.

For one thing, observing some common big-woods food sources, such as overgrown meadows and clear-cuts, is not only possible, but also highly recommended. Additionally, once leaf-off occurs, one can often get up high and observe the woodlands below. Yes, that means sacrificing a hunting opportunity, but it can be well worth it.

When performing long-range observations, employing several tips can be very helpful. The first group revolves around keeping deer ignorant of these activities. Before blundering out, analyze the area to be observed and carefully select a location that will lend itself to helping you remain undetected. That translates to keeping the deer upwind at all times and having enough cover to keep you hidden.

Personally, I find pop-up blinds very valuable for hiding me during observations. In less than a minute, a high-quality blind can be slapped up and ready to use. The cover and ability to move they provide are some of the little things that can make a difference.

Another factor in remaining undetected is getting in and out. When practical, select vantage points that you can reach by crossing as little deer habitat as possible. Not only does this limit the risk of bumping deer, but it also minimizes the odds of them picking up any scent that may have been left behind.

Take the same scent-reduction steps that you would before going hunting. Even when everything is set up perfectly, deer have a tendency to show up where they aren't supposed to, and wind directions change. Having observation efforts educate deer to being hunted is a deadly sin that can greatly reduce your odds of eventual salvation—harvesting the buck.

Selecting observation posts that offer a good field of view is also important. Good fields of view can mean either complete coverage of the area or zoning in on a specific spot. For example, if forced to choose between seeing 90% of a field or watching the 10% that's hidden in a corner, it's often better to watch the 10%.

Speaking of watching effectively, a good spotting scope is extremely helpful. Though binoculars can work, once light begins to fade, a spotting scope's extra magnification can make the difference between positively identifying a spectacular buck or discerning that it's only a large-bodied deer.

Finally, when a targeted buck is seen, note the trail he's using. This may sound basic, but it's easy to get so caught up in the animal that the details are lost. Once the animal is spotted, find a landmark that will allow you to pinpoint his location later. Employing these tips can make observations far less disruptive and far more beneficial.

When used properly, scouting cameras can be excellent tools for revealing the bucks on a particular property and giving you insights into their patterns.

LOCATING MR. BIG WITH CAMERAS

As shown by Larry Kline's success, trail cameras can be powerful and beneficial tools. That is, assuming they are quality units and used properly.

I have no doubt that any deer has the potential to be trained to accept a flash and noisy camera as harmless. Some don't even seem to care the first time they experience an up-close photo session with these potentially harmful units. However, some mature bucks have no tolerance for anything out of the norm and won't stick around for the training session. Though they most likely won't abandon the area, they are apt to avoid the location where the camera is set. I've seen this firsthand.

When choosing a scouting camera, I look for several features. First, above all else, it must be quiet. Camera noise is unacceptable. Next is reliability. If I'm going to base decisions on what a camera reports, it better not misfire or miss shots. That also encompasses the triggering time. A second may not seem to be much time, but if it takes that long to snap

Setting scouting cameras behind the scrape and shooting out over it captures both the bucks working the scrape and many of the deer investigating it from a distance.

a photo, an amazingly high number of rear-end shots will be the result. Though one can easily argue both sides of whether a standard flash scares deer, I prefer an infrared flash. It has the ability to capture more readable night photos at a distance, and is undetectable to deer. Finally, I can't even imagine ever using a film-based scouting camera again. Digital is simply so much easier, faster and cheaper than having to develop film.

My next great concerns involve the users. Though checking pictures is fun, every time we step into the woods, we are leaving sign of our activities. Repeatedly checking those cameras can be very harmful to our hunting efforts.

Cleaning the camera, taking odor-control steps, avoiding trails, and timing the trips during mid-day hours are steps in the right direction. Next, apply my three-strikes rule: After setup, I refuse to take more than two more trips to the camera location. Commonly, I'll return a week after setup and yank the unit then. After all, if Mr. Big hasn't passed within seven days, I probably don't want to hunt that location anyway. Occasionally, I'll either leave it one more week or I'll reset the camera there later to see if the buck's patterns now include that area. However, I'll never make more than three consecutive trips to the same location.

To break down placement techniques, let's look at three examples of sites to monitor: food and water sources, trails and scrapes.

A very quick and effective way to get an idea of the caliber of animals living in an area is to monitor prime food and water sources. Begin by placing a scouting camera at sites that show the heaviest signs of feeding or watering. If the area is too large for one setup to do it justice, either employ more than one or relocate the unit after a week or two. After covering one food or water source, move to the next. Even on relatively large properties, this rotation scheme provides very good coverage in just one or two months.

When food sources aren't a good option, scouting units can be set up on trails. In this case, setting the scouting camera about four or five yards off to the side, with its coverage area cutting across the trail, is far less intrusive than aiming it down the trail.

Finally, there's the scrape method. Because many scrapes are worked after dark, and a high percentage of them are used sporadically at best, scrape hunting can be a very frustrating experience. Trail monitors certainly can't guarantee success, but they can at least tell us that a mature buck is working the scrape and whether the activity ever occurs during shooting hours.

Setting the camera behind the scrape, so that it shoots out over the scrape and also covers deer passing by in front of it, is commonly the best placement. That way, you'll capture pictures of deer working and many just investigating the scrape.

When using all of these placement strategies, my primary goals are to find the buck I'm after, note the time he's there, and find his track. To help locate tracks on trails, I'll often rake a small portion clean of debris. It may surprise some to note that I rely far more heavily on scouting units to locate my buck and get his track than for patterning.

TRACKING BUCKS

Tracks are what I rely on most for gathering details on a specific buck's pattern. Whether I saw him first during observations or in a photograph, one of my primary goals is to then scour the area and find his track.

When I locate a track, measuring the length and width of the hoof, along with a tip to dewclaw and stride measurement when possible, gives me the foundation of the buck's fingerprint. Taking it a step further by noting the shape of the tip, chips in the hoof and any other visible characteristics, I can now track that animal almost anywhere it goes. Of course, the four hooves are not identical, but their size and overall shape characteristics are usually close enough to generate a match.

The ability to track a buck is extremely beneficial. Let's say that in early September we document the track of an animal we spotted in an alfalfa field. Later we find a track leading from a bed and pull out the tape, along with our track notes. Just that quick, we can often identify the animal. In October, we find the same track in a line of scrapes along the edge of a swamp. November turns another up in the bean field a mile away.

The point is that when tracks are documented, they can fill in a lot of the missing puzzle pieces required for patterning that buck of a lifetime. Literally, anywhere that buck leaves a track, we can tell that he was there.

Many green fields and trails don't provide adequate surfaces for collecting tracks but, luckily, simply clearing the litter from a three-foot section of the trail will correct that. Now we no longer have to guess if that buck is using a specific trail. He will show us for certain. By scrubbing it clean periodically, we can even tell how regularly he travels it.

Most often kicking a patch clear with a rubber boot is enough. To do an even better job, a garden rake can be used. This not only clears the trail, but also breaks the soil to provide an even better medium for collecting tracks. When all else fails, dirt can be brought in to improve conditions that simply won't work otherwise.

"Track catchers" are so powerful that they are the reason I don't rely heavily on scouting cameras as patterning tools. Not only are track catchers free, but I can place as many as I need at any given time. That allows me to blanket an area one time, come back a week later and, in one shot, have all the answers I need.

It isn't unusual for a hunter to be able to pinpoint the trail a buck uses to enter a food source. Unfortunately, it's also common for the trail, as it works back into the woods toward bedding areas, to split into several branches. That leaves the hunter guessing which bedding area the buck is using.

Armed with a rake, the hunter can create a track catcher on the main trail and just up from each split. Returning a week later, he can check the main trail for the buck's track. If it's there, he can check the track catchers on the splinter trails. Based on which one holds tracks, the hunter now knows one of the locations where Mr. Big is bedding.

Simply put, strategically positioned track catchers throughout a habitat are invaluable tools for monitoring the activity of a fingerprinted buck. Any time you question if the animal is using a trail, crossing, funnel or almost any confined area, track catchers can provide the answer.

As with the scouting cameras, care must be used to minimize disturbances. Using the three-strike rule, avoiding stepping on trails, cutting odors, and only going in at mid-day, when deer are most likely bedded, all are important steps. Following these guidelines, you will receive the full benefits from this patterning tactic.

FOLLOWING IN HIS FOOTSTEPS

In areas that receive a blanket of snow, a buck's entire world becomes a giant track catcher. A day or two after a fresh snowfall, getting out and finding the targeted buck's track provides an incredible opportunity to nail down precisely what he has been doing. All one must do is follow his trail backwards.

Taking that direction ensures that the buck isn't reacting to your pressure and that he was indeed moving naturally. From this natural movement, you can easily identify his travel routes, food sources, bedding sites and anything he may have done.

Granted, even following the trail backwards is no guarantee that you won't bump into the monarch, which definitely makes this an aggressive and somewhat risky in-season tactic. However, when nothing else seems to be working, time is running out and you don't know where he is, it can lead to results.

Luckily, bumping him once typically won't kill your chances. Bucks seldom alter their long-term patterns based on one relatively harmless encounter with humans. On the plus side, bumping him in this way alerts you that his pattern is relatively stable and that it's advisable to modify hunting strategies immediately to capitalize on your findings.

Backtracking in the first weeks after season ends eliminates any concern, but it does require a little more analysis. Assuming his survival, along with no major changes occurring to the habitat or with food sources, chances are very good that the buck will be following those patterns next late season. The real question becomes whether he does the same things during the earlier phases of season; that's where woodsmanship and common sense help to provide answers.

Backtracking a buck in the snow can reveal everything the buck did for as long as the track can be followed, and provide priceless insight into his life.

For example, if old rubs happen to be intermittently marking his travels, chances are good that he used that same route earlier in the year. Some food sources, such as soybeans, sorghum and corn, are used for much of season. However, if the area holds only alfalfa fields buried under the snow and he happens to be feeding on woody browse, chances are strong that he'll be feeding on alfalfa during much of next year's season. Also, relatively short-lived food sources, such as mast crops, must be figured into the equation. Still, even if all these findings only produce his patterns for next late season, they put the hunter much farther ahead of where he previously was.

RECORD KEEPING

Another important and often-overlooked aspect of patterning bucks lies in record keeping. The logs I keep are grouped into two categories. One covers my overall hunting activities, including scouting notes, such as locations that show deer activities and places I want to check in further detail. In many ways, this is much like a journal, summarizing what I found and want to remember for the future.

I also log deer sightings and the details of each hunt. Regardless of whether it's an afternoon conducting long-range observations or a morning on the stand, the entry begins with a description of exactly where I was posted and how I got in and out. It then includes details on the conditions, including temperature, wind direction and speed, cloud cover, notes on any precipitation that may occur and the moon phase. As of late, I've even begun including barometric pressure, and whether it's rising, falling or constant.

Next comes the information on the stars of the show. I try to include a description of each deer I see, naming them if they have recognizable traits. I include what time period I observed them, where they were and what they were doing, all in specific detail.

For example, instead of merely noting that I saw a young buck feeding, I'd write that I saw a 2.5-year-old eight-point, scoring approximately 100 inches. He entered the field five minutes before sunset—specific references to sunset and sunrise provide a better timeline than citing the hour on the clock—from the trail in the northeast corner. He spent the first eight minutes eating acorns under the cluster of oaks before feeding his way steadily out to the middle of the alfalfa field.

I include the same sort of notes in my logs on specific bucks—logs dedicated exclusively to the activities of individual animals. Having one source of information on each buck is more effective than sifting through the general logs in an attempt to find information specific to him. Because these logs are kept on my laptop, I also copy them into my general logs. That makes it easy for me to maintain a master general hunting log file and then break that into logs for each property I hunt.

The final piece of the puzzle to truly patterning a mature buck comes from plotting his sign and sightings on a map. Granted, it may be impossible to pattern him during the rut, but with the aid of a map, we can come pretty darn close to nailing him down during the other phases of season.

For any phase of season, filling in every gap of a buck's life strictly from our findings is a tremendous challenge. However, when it is mapped out, along with plotting a property's thick protective cover and food and water sources, it's much easier to apply educated guesses and deductive reasoning to piece things together.

To make it better still, marking our findings on three clear overlays—one for early season, the lull and scraping phase; another for the chase and breeding phases; and the last for post rut and second rut—gives us the opportunity to see how his patterns change throughout the season. With that, we can compare and contrast each phase, gaining valuable insight into the best stand locations for each.

DIVIDING YOUR EGGS INTO SEVERAL BASKETS

Even with all of this, finding more than one buck is extremely helpful. A lot can happen to mess up bucks that seem practically gift-wrapped. Locating more than one gives you a safety net in case things go haywire.

My own experience several seasons ago is a good example of that. In the days leading up to the opener, I'd located five good bucks, two of which were living on land open to public hunting. The other three were calling a parcel of heavily hunted private land home. Though the ground was restricted, as many as five hunters could be found sitting in various trees at one time.

With a pretty good handle on all the bucks' patterns, my stands were set and I was ready for the opening day. Knowing that the largest, a 10-point I'd estimated in the low 160s, routinely fed in a small grassy meadow, I began the season there.

Sitting in stand that first afternoon, I was more than a little disappointed to spot three other hunters. With a smidge more than an hour of shooting light left, they drove their ATVs into the meadow and started snooping around for places to hang their stands. Amazingly, though the meadow was just over an acre in size, they never saw me slip my stand out of the tree and make the long walk back to my truck. Before opening day was over, I knew the location would be trashed beyond repair. Such is life when competing with others on hunting grounds.

With four bucks still remaining on my list, the following afternoon found me targeting the one feeding on the oak ridge. Though also on public lands, I was confident that I'd have the ridge to myself. The acorn drop in the area was early and very light that year. Because the ridge was a pain to get to, as well as the rest of the oak woods being void of acorns, I didn't believe other hunters had put in the work to find this secluded patch. I was right.

It wasn't long before the ridge was covered in deer. With ample shooting light left, I spotted the large eight-point cresting the ridge. He was well out of range, but I watched him feed until dark. Since the area was covered in does and fawns, I didn't dare risk attempting to call him within range.

Over the next week, I hunted the stand three more times. With so many deer feeding on the limited acorns, I knew the location would be picked dry fast. That knowledge, as well as a low-impact route to and from my stand, convinced me to hunt the location hard. So long as I could keep the deer ignorant, I would continue to hunt the ridge until they exhausted the acorn supply. After one more close encounter with the eight, and just over a week into season, the acorns were gone. Not surprisingly, the large eight vanished with them.

During the period of time I was hunting the acorns, I was also alternating trips to the private land. I even passed on a shot opportunity at the smaller of the three bucks I'd targeted, because the other two more impressive bucks were flirting with the edge of my shooting range at the time.

Just under two weeks in, with the desire to fill my tag growing stronger, I shifted to hunting the 3.5-year-old nine-point—the same buck I'd passed the week before. As luck would have it, a well-placed stand delivered an easy shot opportunity. A short tracking job later and the buck was mine.

Finding and targeting more than one buck was key to that season's success. As of writing this, in three of the past four seasons I've been able to tag out early. During each of the three seasons I was successful, I'd located two or more mature bucks to hunt. Though few of us have enough access to private lands to do that, adding public lands to the equation makes it possible for nearly anyone.

CONCLUSION

Truly patterning a buck takes work and scouting smart, but it can be accomplished. The tools described here can all be extremely helpful. However, I'd be lying to you if I claimed that I've ever used all of them together on a single deer. Personally, I rely on observations, sign, track catchers and my logs far more than scouting cameras and mapping sign. Still, all are great tools for hunters to have at their disposal, to be used as needed.

In fairness, I must also point out that one rarely knows every detail about any buck. The majority of the time, patterning involves discovering small pieces of a buck's life and using that info to generate educated guesses on how to most effectively hunt him.

Further complicating matters is that buck patterns rarely stay the same throughout the season. As discussed in Chapter 5, many changes occur over the course of season to both a buck and his habitat. Because of that, when a kink in a buck's armor is found, hunt it smart and fast, before his patterns shift.

Follow that advice and use these tools, and you just may accomplish the ultimate in bowhunting deer. Effectively patterning and arrowing a specific buck takes your game to the next level—to the apex of the sport. ∎

When used properly, scouting cameras can be excellent tools for revealing the bucks on a particular property and giving you insights into their patterns.

10. Hunting the Wind: What Most "Experts" Won't Tell You

As we approached the downed 146 4/8-inch 10-point, I exchanged high fives with my good friend Tom Indrebo. At first glance, it was one of those rare bucks that had fallen in place almost effortlessly. I knew his bedding sites, food sources and routes connecting them. Based on the wind direction, I could even predict the route he'd take on a given day. I had the buck nailed.

When most hunters speak of hunting the wind, they are referring to keeping the deer upwind of their stands. That's understandable. Not allowing deer to enter their odor stream is a prerequisite to having a successful hunt. However, there are already ample teaching resources available to instruct hunters on how to safely hunt the wind. Heck, I covered it some myself in my first book. Furthermore, if you remember Chapter 4, you already know

For Tom Indrebo and me, determining how this buck was using the wind for protection was a key to harvesting him.

that I don't worry about having bucks downwind, so I'm not going to cover all that here.

Instead, I'll invest this space in discussing how bucks use the wind and how we can use that to our advantage. For the life of me, I have no clue why this aspect of hunting the wind isn't covered in more detail. Bowhunting pioneers Gene and Barry Wensel are the only others I'm aware of who ever tackled the subject in any real depth.

I'm not pointing this out to say no one else has ever truly covered it. It is possible that they have and it slipped by me. My true purpose for bringing this up is to provide a belated yet very sincere thank-you to the Wensel brothers. I stumbled across their lessons on hunting the wind when I was still in my early stages of bowhunting. They helped me take my game to a new level.

Learning how bucks use the wind is one of those little details that truly can make that much of a difference. When reading the rest of this chapter, remember that deer rely much more heavily on their noses than humans ever could. In many ways, their sense of smell is every bit as important to them as our eyes and ears are to us. Sure, on a small level, deer communicate through grunts and bleats, and they relate to the world visually. However, they really talk to each other through odors. They may question their other senses. They rarely doubt what their noses tell them.

USING THE WIND FOR SAFETY'S SAKE

To illustrate how bucks use the wind in their routine, everyday activities, let's look more closely at how the taking of the 10-point Tom and I were celebrating at the beginning of this chapter came together.

It really all began in early August, when Indrebo gave me a farm to rip apart for his clients and myself. It offered two major sources of cover. One was a strip of woods that followed a meandering creek slicing through a crop valley. The other was a large, steep-wooded ridge flanked on both sides by crop fields. Studying the topo maps, I found several likely locations for later in season. However, I knew the only way to pick early-season stands would be to observe the crop fields.

Because of the setting, observing with a spotting scope from the truck was the best approach. I could watch one valley until just about dark and then flip to the other side for a quick viewing. I saw the 10-point buck feeding in the north valley that first time in.

To be more specific, my logs show that the temps were in the high 60s, the skies were partly cloudy and the wind was out of the southeast. I spotted a total of three does, five fawns and three bucks feeding on the alfalfa in the north valley. Two bucks were yearlings and the other was the

10.   The south valley held two does, three fawns and two yearling bucks.

Over the course of repeated observations, I saw two bucks that would score higher than the 10 and another that was slightly below. To be honest, the reason I targeted the 10 was because of his regular appearances.

Taking it a step further, my logs also showed that he used the wind direction to select which valley he visited for feeding. When winds came from northerly directions, he selected the north valley. Conversely, he fed in the south valley when winds had southern origins. Putting that together, I believed I had a good chance at arrowing him.

Mid-day, still a couple of weeks before season's opening, I set out to place stands to take him. I'd already noted the areas where he entered the field on both sides of the ridge. The problem was that, though they were relatively close, he didn't use the same trails each time. It was entirely possible that I could get the side right, but have the buck enter the field out of bow range.

Because of that, I decided to conduct one hard scouting and stand-hanging trip. With two stands strapped to my back, I began walking the edge of the woods along the south valley. Mid-ridge, a point dropped off the side to serve as a natural route between the food and the bedding on top. Based on his field-entry points, I believed it was a good bet that he was traveling that point. I was not disappointed. In fact, I traced the buck's old rub line all the way up the point to his bed. With large tracks indicating the line was still active, I knew I was onto something good.

Surveying the area, a large oak was positioned perfectly on the crest of the point, providing an easy shot to the rub line. With a low-impact route in and the tree being only 150 yards from his bed, I hung the first stand in the oak.

When further scouting revealed a second bedding site and rub line, suddenly it all made sense. The buck was bedding on knobs jutting from opposite sides of the ridge. With a wind from the south, he would bed on the north side. That enabled him to use his nose to detect danger approaching from on top of the ridge and use his eyes to scan for danger lurking on the ridge side below. Then, late afternoon, he could rise, crest the ridge and drop into the south valley. That way, as he approached the field, he could keep the wind in his face and scent the food source for danger. When the wind had a northern angle, he could bed on the south side and mirror this action in the other direction. In either case, he was using the wind to keep himself safe to the fullest extent.

On both sides, he followed his trail from his bed down most of the ridge side. As he neared the field, he'd break off to use one of several trails to enter the food source. I believe these various routes were selected to fully utilize his sense of smell. In other words, he'd finish his entry to the field by taking whichever splinter trail allowed him to scent-check the field best under the current wind direction.

After slapping up a stand on the opposite side, just before the trail broke, I was set. Returning to the farm early in the season, a quick check of the wind told me which stand to sit. To be safe, I climbed into the stand extra early. Even with the day producing high winds and the breeding phase still a long way off, I knew being so close to the bedding area could lead to early movement.

It all started coming together a full hour before dark. Catching movement out of the corner of my eye, I saw the mature 10-point trotting down his now freshened rub line.

Already positioned, I was ready when the buck stepped out from under the oak's branch. Settling the pin high behind the front shoulder, I sent the arrow driving into the buck's vitals. He crashed away, but I knew he wouldn't go far.

Of course, this situation was more cut-and-dried than most. In settings with limited food or cover, if bucks only fed when they could travel into the wind to get to food, they'd eventually die of starvation. Along those lines, there are other times when a buck simply wants to feed on acorns worse than he wants to eat browse in a clear-cut. If traveling from his bedding site to the acorns involves walking with the wind at his back, he'll do it more often than not.

However, knowing that they'd prefer to walk directly into or quartering into the wind is information that hunters can use to their advantage. All else being equal, keeping that in mind when selecting which stand to sit can up the odds of meeting Mr. Big on a given day.

On the flip side, bucks almost always use the wind when deciding how and where to bed. At the very least, they have the strong tendency to bed with the wind at their back and use their eyes to protect their front side. That makes sense from a survival standpoint.

This knowledge can be applied in broken or rolling land. When a buck is rotating between several bedding sites, the wind direction can dictate which he selects. The safety advantage of beds that simultaneously offer a good view of the front and wind coverage of the back is tremendous. Applying that knowledge makes it much easier to predict where a buck will bed and what stand sites are most likely to produce encounters with him during his travels to likely food sources.

In a nutshell, outside of during the chase and breeding phases of season, buck movement is mostly between bedding and food and water. When one doesn't have a good reason to select one stand site over another, analyze which covers the trail that provides a buck the ability to use the wind most to his advantage. Though that won't always lead to sitting on the right trail, it will far more often than strictly relying on random luck.

LOVE IS IN THE AIR

As helpful as playing the wind during the non-rut related phases of season can be, it's even more so during the scraping, chase and breeding phases. That is when hunters can gain an incredible advantage.

Many of the best-producing scrapes are those located on the downwind side of bedding areas. With a single pass, a buck can check both his scrape and the bedding area for a doe entering estrus early. In that scenario, it isn't a coincidence that the hottest scrapes on a given day are often dictated by the wind direction.

To fine-tune stand placement for hunting these scrapes, I strive to set up 20 yards downwind of them. Any buck that wants to check the scrape must either come to it or pass downwind of it. It isn't uncommon for bucks to check these scrapes from 10-40 yards downwind. Such a stand placement

When determining how to set up on doe-bedding areas, start by selecting the downwind side.

allows me to catch all of that activity. More than once, this strategy has provided me with shot opportunities at bucks checking scrapes from a distance.

As helpful as the wind is for checking scrapes, it's even more advantageous for checking does. Though bucks may seem to be moving at random during the rut, there is often method to their madness. To maximize their breeding opportunities, bucks must effectively cruise as many doe concentrations as is practical in a swift and efficient manner. The wind is a tremendous aid in accomplishing that.

For example, as opposed to running wildly around a field, sniffing doe after doe, one pass on the downwind side of the field lets the buck know if any are ready. While doing so, he can also scent-check the trails for any hot does that have recently entered or exited the field.

All of this makes the downwind side of prime food sources a good place to sit. To further stack the odds, stands placed 15-20 yards in, off the inside corners of these fields, can be great choices. The hunter can cover the bucks cruising the edge as deep as 40 yards inside the woods, intercept those walking the actual edge of the field as well as any bucks that may be following a doe on the worn trails entering the field that most inside corners possess.

Bucks often cut just inside those corners when getting from one side of the field to the other. Doing this provides the quickest route that offers the safety of cover. All of these things can be taken advantage of when hunting the downwind corners of fields that are being used as food sources.

Finally, as was the case while scraping, running the downwind edges of doe-bedding areas is the most effective means for a buck to scent-check the bedded does. Placing stands 20 yards off the edge, covering the best entrance/exit trail, positions the hunter to intercept most of this movement, as well as providing the chance that a hot doe will lead a buck past the stand.

The story of an Illinois buck I took is a good example of how this can pay off. During a spring scouting trip, I'd found an area where the mature woods had been selectively logged. One patch along a ridge finger had been logged harder than the rest. The combination of the thicker regrowth, extra downed tops and view of the more open creek bottom below all resulted in a prime family-group bedding area.

On the surface, it seemed like bucks could be working it from any side. However, further analysis revealed that the wind direction would be the key. When the wind blew down the point, it created one best route for roaming bucks. By skirting the lower edge, they could scent-check all the does, the bedding area, and use their eyes to scan the creek bottom below.

The first November morning providing this wind found me in that stand. My sit was short and sweet.

By factoring in what wind directions would make the stand location the best, I was able to take this wide, high-beamed nine-point on the stand's first sit.

Around 8 a.m., the large-bodied, high-beamed nine-pointer appeared. As I had hoped, he was skirting the lower edge of the thicket. Coming in on a string, his head alternated between tilting up to check the wind and turning back to use his eyes to scan the creek bottom below.

At about 30 yards out, I drew and settled my knuckle behind my ear. Coming to a stop, he intently scanned the creek bottom for does. Turning just a bit as he did, I let the arrow fly. As the arrow sank in, the buck took flight for the creek bottom. Folding as he neared the bank, the wide, chocolate-racked buck was mine.

USING SCENT WITH THE WIND TO SEAL THE DEAL

In some situations, bedding areas are too large or don't offer one obvious spot to set up. That's when one pulls out the scent to help focus deer activity around the stand. This is exactly what I did to create a focal point while hunting an otherwise non-focused bedding area in big timber.

Lying between a creek bottom and ridge top, right in the middle of a large stand of timber, was a large doe-bedding area. One problem with the setup was that the bedding area went on for nearly a half-mile and held numerous potentially good stand locations, but not one that would cover the majority of bucks cruising by. The other problem was that bucks were also running the valley on the opposite side of the ridge.

Applying how bucks use the wind to your scent strategies makes scents far more effective. Scents can even be used to reel in bucks before they hit the hunter's odor stream.

For the best odds, I needed to do something to concentrate the buck activity near my stand. On my way in for the first morning's sit, with the wind blowing up and over the ridge from the bedding area, I paused on top of the ridge to place an estrous urine-soaked scent wick. Reaching to place the wick on a high branch, my hope was that the alluring odors would filter down the other side of the ridge. The goal was to draw bucks up from that valley, but not allow them to locate the source of the odor.

Drawing bucks to the top of the ridge was a good start. Still, because the ridge top was out of shooting range, I needed to lure them farther to get the shot. To do this, I placed two more wicks at 20 yards on both sides of the stand, forming a scent triangle.

Now I had a chance of drawing deer to my stand from the opposite side of the ridge. Upon reaching the top, with the two flanking wicks producing odors, chances were good that, if the buck traveled down the ridge in either direction, he would pick up one of their odor streams and be lured in for the shot. Furthermore, the wicks should draw in any bucks simply cruising the ridge. In either case, they would already be looking for hot does. The scent would simply sell a buck the lie that one was in the bedding area waiting for him to come get her.

Less than an hour after shooting light emerged, I spotted the 150-inch buck on the ridge top. Feverishly scent-checking the air, it was obvious that he was intent on locating the doe whose scent had drawn him up the ridge. With the odor now wafting above his nose, he eventually gave up and began walking the ridge top away from my stand.

His defeatist attitude changed quickly the moment he hit the odor stream of estrous scent from the wick flanking the left side of my stand. He was coming in on a rope; I prepared for the shot. Less than 10 minutes later, as I walked over to where I saw the buck crumble, I was thankful that I'd gone the extra mile in using scent to take advantage of how cruising bucks use the wind.

RELYING SOLELY ON THE WIND

In fairness to those who are either unable or unwilling to take odor control to the extreme, I should point out ways they too can use these techniques.

Under most of these settings, stands can be placed to take advantage of the way bucks use winds, while still being positioned so that the wind blows from the stand at an angle, quartering toward, but not directly across the buck's most likely approach routes. Granted, because winds often shift and bucks don't always show up where they're supposed to, this is riskier than taking odor control to the extreme. Additionally, there will be many wind conditions that make this approach too risky for a stand site. However, multiple stands can be set to increase the likelihood of a huntable quartering wind occurring.

Another option, when hunting scrapes, feeding locations and doe-bedding areas, is placing stands downwind of where one believes the buck will pass. Unfortunately, because these cruises only occur frequently during the scrape, chase and breeding phases of season, well-established trails don't often exist. Instead, the hunter is hunting a more general area downwind of a point of interest. Because bucks are more randomly passing through the general area, relying on staying downwind of most bucks to remain undetected usually translates into a comparatively higher percentage passing through so far upwind that they're out of shooting range.

Still, this technique and placement strategy can work. For example, let's look at applying this to intercepting bucks scent-checking the downwind side of bedding areas. If the most likely path skirts 20 yards from the edge, placement 35 yards from the edge will work. Now you can safely cover the path, as well as have decent odds of the odors flowing over the heads of bucks that pass just downwind of the stand.

When hunting scrapes, placing the stand 40 yards downwind is often safe and will intercept many of the bucks checking from downwind. Though it doesn't provide a shot to the scrape, a grunt or two may lure those bucks into range.

Scent can also be used to our advantage. Placing scent out 20 yards from both sides of the stand can potentially reel bucks cruising downwind before they hit the hunter's odor stream. Of course, it's also always possible to coax those that are too far upwind closer for the shot with a grunt or doe call.

Hunting upwind of a buck's bedding site is the trickiest. Even using a quartering wind, chances are high that it will momentarily shift to the bedding site. That shift can be disastrous. The trick is setting up far enough away from the bedded buck to remain undetected through the wind shifts. The farther an odor travels, the less likely it becomes that the currents will deliver it to a buck's nostrils, and the more it dissipates before it arrives. Although bucks can smell objects from 500 yards away, odds are good that the distance will stop him from picking you up when a rogue shift in wind direction occurs.

Though taking odor control to the extreme makes these techniques easier and more successful, relying on the wind to keep you safe can be effective. The cost is placing a higher premium on choosing a stand location that's better for the hunter's wind than the buck's ability to use it.

CONCLUSION

Learning to take advantage of how bucks use the wind may not receive much exposure, but it sure provides the savvy hunter with a tremendous advantage. As a matter of fact, that just may be why it's barely, if ever, covered in detail. Because of its effectiveness, perhaps the "experts" who have picked up on its power want to guard this secret for themselves. If you give it a try, you just may begin to understand why. ■

11. Tricks to Making Almost Every Tree-Stand Location Work

My cameraman, an accomplished hunter himself, sat perched 30-some feet up a tree. The day before, he and I had been scouting this new piece of land. From the topo map, it was apparent that this bench showed promise. Positioned halfway up a very steep ridge, it ran a solid mile. With numerous bedding areas sprinkled on top of the ridge and heavy feeding activity occurring in the valley below, it was obvious that this was a prime chase-and-breeding-phase stand site. Bucks were certain to be cruising back and forth, checking the bench for the scent trails of hot does.

While hunting the stand several days later, several hundred yards away, my cameraman caught a glimpse of movement coming down the ridge. Cradled between three tall, thin oaks, he positioned himself and readied the camera equipment. Zooming in, he judged the buck to easily go in the 160s. Maintaining the path the trotting monster was taking, he would pass within chip-shot range of the stand. After positioning the camera to record the likely shot location, he grabbed his bow and readied himself. As the monster trotted to 27 paces from his stand, it froze and stared directly at him. Frozen still with the buck quartering toward him, he had no choice but to wait out the inevitable outcome. Moments later, the buck twirled and dashed away, leaving him with nothing but a moment recorded on video to show for the experience.

Since I first began bowhunting, the rules of stand concealment have changed. Back in the mid-'70s, I could get away with most anything, provided I was 15 or more feet up in a tree. The deer I was chasing just weren't used to looking up for danger. The idea of concealment was nothing more than an afterthought to me. As the years passed, this gradually changed to the point that I now take stand concealment very seriously. To consistently avoid being busted by old does and mature bucks, I believe it is something that must be adequately addressed.

Over the years, as both bow- and stand-hunting became more popular across the country, the deer naturally have become more wary of objects lurking in the branches. Thinking about it, it makes all the sense in the world. The natural selection of any prey species ensures that the ones that are able to adapt survive. Don't get me wrong; there are still locations where simply getting up in a tree is three-fourths of the battle, but they are diminishing rapidly.

I'm also not saying that there aren't a few dumb deer in just about any setting, but they seldom reach maturity. Deer in the majority of this country simply don't live to old age if they're not a cut above the rest, and those are almost always the ones that I'm chasing. All this has resulted in the need for me to develop an effective stand-concealment strategy.

Before we get farther, I'd like to take a moment to address something. For those who purchased my first book, *Advanced Stand Hunting Strategies*, I'm sure that you've noticed that I went out of my way not to simply rehash the same topics in this book. I feel that doing so would cheat the reader. Let's face it, even when new hunts are used as anecdotes and the words explaining the techniques are rewritten, the message remains the same and little new is offered.

Since *Advanced Stand Hunting Strategies* contains a similar chapter to this, I was initially very hesitant to redo it for this book. After debating it long and hard in my mind, I obviously ultimately decided to include it. Sure, part of my justification for this is that I've picked up an additional tip or two and significantly expanded on the topic, dedicating this chapter solely to making tree stands work effectively and the next chapter to hunting on the ground.

However, the main reason is that I simply can't get over the number of stands I find on public lands that I refuse to believe hunters can arrow deer from. It shocks me that so many hunters, including a surprising number of seasoned veterans, don't understand that sitting 12-feet-up a telephone pole like tree, no more than three yards off the trail, isn't a great idea. I'll tell you what, if the hunters who are hanging these stands are able to go undetected in them, then they're obviously much better at it than I am. Being as careful as possible, I'd be lucky to get past half the immature deer that pass by, and I don't even want to think about how many mature does and bucks would bust me.

Along with this, I'm being approached by more of my seminar attendees today seeking advice on how to make stand locations work, as well as receiving more questions about ground-blind use than ever before. The final straw is that each year, more and more bowhunters seem to forget that it's possible to take whitetails by doing nothing more than hiding behind some brush. Because of that, many great stand sites are either ruined by sitting in small, coverless trees or blown off as unhuntable. All of that has made me painfully aware of the need to continue covering this topic.

Selecting large trees, with ample back cover, that are out of the deer's direct line of sight provides dramatically better odds of going undetected.

DEFINING THE PERFECT TREE

To begin with, we need to quickly cover what an ideal tree to hang a stand consists of. First, even for those who are confident in their odor-fighting abilities, it's best if the tree is on the downwind side of where the deer are most likely to appear.

Furthermore, it shouldn't be on top of the deer or too far away. If the stand is much less than 10 yards from where the deer are likely to be, the first issue is that the shot angle will be needlessly sharp. That results in higher odds of a dreaded single-lung hit.

The next issue to being on top of deer is that the stand is likely to be within the deer's direct line of sight as they approach the stand. Being in that direct line of sight makes it more likely that they'll detect something unnatural in the tree.

Positioned off to the side, between 15 and 30 yards away, is ideal for me. I'm very comfortable shooting up to 50 yards, but from over 30 things must be perfect. An ideal range for most probably falls in the 10- to 20-yard range. Remember, you want to be back off, but still close enough to make it feel like a chip shot. That makes the ideal distance dependent on the hunter's comfort range.

Being a right-handed shooter, I also strive to have the deer action be on my left side, which requires the minimum shifting in the stand to position my body for the shot. For left-handed shooters, having the action on the right minimizes movement.

Next, one should consider the sun. Ideally, the hunter should remain in the shadows to further hide movement. Along with that, keeping the sun out of your eyes is very helpful for seeing into the shadows. If the sun is shining directly in the hunter's eyes and the deer is in the shadows, the sun goes from being a hassle to making it impossible to shoot. I know. I've lived that situation. When placing the tree stand, consider if it will be a morning, afternoon or all-day hunting location. Factoring that in allows the stand to be placed to keep the sun out of the hunter's eyes.

Lastly, the tree should provide enough cover to break the hunter's silhouette. Without that, even the movement of drawing the bow can be easily detected. Oh, and it should go without saying that the tree is alive and that the stand is either level or leaning slightly backward. Putting stands in dead trees or at an angle tilting to the side or down toward the ground is risking death.

STAND HEIGHT VS. BACK COVER

With that out of the way, let's start looking at some more specific considerations. To begin with, along with being off the deer's direct line of sight, I've found that having quality back cover is the most critical aspect of allowing for undetected movement and not getting silhouetted. I know many swear by extreme stand height, and I've heard numerous successful hunters claim that you just can't consistently take a trophy unless you are at least 20, 25 and even in excess of 30 feet up. Well, if you will recall, my cameraman was kissing the clouds when he was busted cold. Although extreme heights are more forgiving, they will not guarantee remaining invisible from a cagey old buck.

I'm not a huge fan of great heights. Rarely will I hang a stand over 30 feet up because of the sharp shot angle it provides. For me, I will take a double lung shot every time. All else being equal, I prefer a height of between 20 and 25 feet up. Heck, I've found that even 12 feet up is acceptable, provided good back cover is present. However, the amount and quality of cover necessary to consistently remain hidden increases the closer to the ground you sit. Using this philosophy, I have been able to harvest the majority of my bucks from around 20 feet high.

When choosing stand height, my primary objective is to find the spot on the tree that will cover my backside best. With an array of objects present behind the hunter, movement and the hunter's image is masked to a much greater extent. Although front cover is good, and something I strive for as well, it tends to get in the way and doesn't do any better job of breaking the silhouette than back cover.

Branches and clumps of trees are the most common producers of quality back cover. The mat of twigs and leaves they have can do an excellent job of breaking a hunter's outline. Deer have very good peripheral vision. They are able to catch even a flicker of movement off to the side because their eyes are offset to the sides of their heads. The weakness of that trait is that their depth perception is not as strong. Deer have a difficult time picking up individual objects when they are embedded in a tangle of branches.

TO CLEAR OR NOT TO CLEAR

A common mistake many hunters make is clearing too many branches around the stand. I suppose the logic is that they are afraid they will be unable to position their bow to get a shot in all directions. However, the end result is all too often removing the cover for their stand to the point where they stand out. The balance between being able to move one's weapon, shoot in a sufficient number of directions and remain covered is a touchy

Refraining from trimming the branches around the stand can go a long way toward keeping hunters from getting silhouetted.

one. After years of being picked off more than I would care to admit, I eventually learned to err on the side of removing less and remaining undetected.

The best example I can give of this occurred in the early '80s. I had my sights set on a fine eight-point. I'd seen him several times working his way through a gentle valley. Unfortunately, there simply was not a suitable tree to hang a stand in. Still, I forced a homemade ladder stand into a cluster of small aspens, against the only one that was barely big enough to support it.

With the stand secured, I began trimming branches. With trails on three sides, I believed I had to have the ability to shoot easily in all directions. Each time I would look at one of the trails, I noticed another branch that may impede my chance to get "the perfect shot." One by one, I removed them until I was convinced that a deer could not sneak through the area without me having a shot opportunity.

After climbing down and clearing a few shooting lanes, I looked up at the stand and was startled to see how open I had left myself. That tangle of branches I'd set my stand against had transformed into an area nearly void of cover. Even back in those early days, I knew this would be a problem, but decided that if I remained motionless I would be able to get by.

The first afternoon I climbed into the ladder stand to hunt, I was brimming with confidence. Having seen the large eight work through the area each time I'd sat in a nearby stand, I was certain that I'd have a shot.

The adrenaline began to pump when I heard a deer trotting through the woods. This feeling quickly began to fade as I heard the fawn cry accompanying the sounds of the trotting deer. Scampering down the trail came a nubbin buck, bawling for its mother. At 50 yards it froze, stared a hole right through me and bolted like a rocket.

To say I felt humbled does not do it justice. At that moment, I knew I was never going to get a poke at that eight-point. I sat there, trying to somehow convince myself that it was still possible, that I could somehow remain undetected by a mature buck, when I couldn't even dupe a mere fawn. The more I churned it over, the sicker I felt. I only saw the eight-point one more time that season. It was during rifle season, and he was riding in the back of the neighbor's truck.

Looking back on it, my misfortune certainly had as much to do with clearing the massive shooting lanes during season as it did with my stand sticking out like a sore thumb. Don't get me wrong, I believe in having a three-foot-wide shooting lane in all four directions from most stands. It's just that creating them during season is rarely a good idea. They're great when prepped in spring, but I believe less intrusive shooting windows are required in season.

On the flip side, regardless of when the stand is hung, I now firmly believe that the less cover directly around the tree that's trimmed the better. Obviously, one must be able to maneuver the bow to get in position. However, it's very rare that I ever trim more than that any more. Most branches can be bent, tied or tucked out of the way, so that they still provide some extra cover. That change in philosophy alone has made a very positive difference for me.

As with the ugly fawn-busting incident, the diameter of the tree is also another factor to take into consideration. The larger the diameter, the easier it is to appear to be part of the tree. Even when decent back cover is present, it can be tough to remain hidden in a spindly tree. Besides, it can be very difficult to get off a shot while the wind sways you from side to side.

Furthermore, depending on the phase of season or how long the stand will be used, the species of tree can be a consideration as well. Many stands that provide a bounty of cover in early October look barren in November. Although fall colors can be beautiful, they signify the beginning of the stripping of cover from most stands in the woods.

Some species of trees do a much better job of holding their leaves than others. Aspen, maples and birch, for example, will shed much sooner than most oaks. In many areas, oaks have a tendency to retain their leaves longer than other deciduous trees. Better yet, the majority of conifers provide almost changeless cover throughout all of season. The benefits of the cover leaves and needles supply are obvious to our goal of remaining hidden.

The last mistake I made was setting up right on top of the deer trails. Because of not being positioned 10 to 30 yards off to the side, I was directly in the deer's line of sight. As it turned out, even if I'd had the eight broadside, all but one possible shot would have required me revolving in the stand to get into position. I have no doubt that I'd been busted silly if I tried.

Frankly, if I could go back and get a do-over, I wouldn't have even climbed into a tree. My odds of taking that buck from the ground would have been infinitely better than trying to work with what I had for trees. However, that's a topic for the next chapter.

CREATING WORKABLE TREES

Before we get into hunting from the ground, we need to look at how we can make many marginal trees work. In a utopian world, a hunter would always find a well-placed tree that possesses all the characteristics to provide excellent stand concealment. Unfortunately, I have yet to find utopia. So, how do we deal with a situation where we just can't find a strategically located tree that provides us with the cover we need? Often, we can remodel a well-placed tree to make it work.

Trying to get away with hunting trees like this is likely to end in waving tails, snorting does and an unhappy hunter. The addition of PMI's Cover System suddenly makes the same stand a more manageable option.

To begin with, we can attach extra branches to a tree. One method of attachment is nailing and/or wiring branches to the trunk. Although helpful, there are several drawbacks to this. First, it's not legal to cut branches on many public grounds and on private land one must seek the owner's permission before doing so. If they have any desire to someday log the property, they often are not particularly high on the idea of nails or wire on their trees.

Besides those issues, it's difficult to securely attach the branches. If the branches aren't secured properly, the first strong wind that comes up wipes out our efforts. Slipping branches into the platform of a grated stand often holds them in place much better and can be a good alternative.

Regardless of the securing method, another issue is that branches have the tendency to lose their leaves or needles after they have been severed from the tree. Conifers and hardwoods, particularly oaks, generally hold their needles and leaves longer than deciduous softwoods. Therefore, they should be used when possible.

My preferred method of increasing cover is to enlist the aid of artificial tools. In today's hunting marketplace, there are several quality products geared to stand concealment. Of the ones I've tried, PMI's Cover System is by far the best option I've found. It's simply a set of six flexible branches that strap to the backside of the tree or front of the tree stand. Once the unit is in place, it can be easily bent into any position that suits the hunter's taste. Just like that, the straightest telephone pole like tree provides instant cover.

Regardless of whether real limbs are used or synthetic systems, as long as the tree is large enough to easily support the stand and doesn't stick out like a sore thumb, it can be made to work. A good rule of thumb to employ is when a tree doesn't provide ample natural cover, imagine what it'd look like with the addition of a squirrel's nest of branches. If that's good enough, make it work. If not, hunt from the ground!

CONCLUSION

Ultimately, the entire point of this chapter can be boiled down into a couple of sentences. When selecting stand sites, remember that seeing deer isn't the only goal. In actuality, there are three goals that must all perform as one: you must see them, go undetected and have the ability to shoot the one you want. Following the guidelines and techniques in this chapter empowers any reader to pull that off a very high percentage of the time. Do that and every last one of you can walk around the woods, shaking your heads in disbelief at other hunter's stand selections.

Lastly, when there isn't a suitable tree where you have to have one, don't force it or walk away from a great spot. Instead, hunt from the ground. As you're about to find out, it's both easy and effective. ■

12. Mastering Hunting from the Ground

I first saw the incredible main frame 10-point standing a mere 20 yards away, as if he materialized out of thin air. With our blind covered in snow and tucked in next to a round bale, the buck that would easily score somewhere above the mid 160s scanned the field, oblivious to our presence. Whispering to my cameraman not to move, I waited for the monster whitetail to spot the decoy placed 50 yards behind the blind. Hidden by the angle, the buck dropped his head and began pawing through the 18 inches of snow cover, exposing the alfalfa that was hidden below.

After he swung his body around to a broadside position and dropped his head to feed, I began to make my move. Already in position, I slowly raised my bow no more than three inches before the slammer's head snapped up and he began staring a hole through me. With just enough time to realize that I needed to be at full draw already to take this animal, two powerful bounds removed him from my life.

I chose to begin this chapter with the events of this painful bowhunt because it effectively illustrates the benefits what the better pop-up blinds on today's market can deliver. After all, I was stuck in a situation where hunting from a tree wasn't an option. The sign showed me the place I had to be and my pop-up blind allowed me to effectively set up there. For several minutes, a grizzled old buck lingered within 20 yards of my blind. Heck, he even stared right past it for nearly a minute, never having a clue that it was out of place. If that doesn't state how effectively blinds can open doors to otherwise nearly unhuntable locations, as well as their ability to help hunters go undetected, I don't know what would.

That hunt also clearly points out the importance of following certain guidelines. The old buck didn't spook at the blind. He spooked at me. Worse yet, it was all my fault. He caught the movement of my uncovered hand. Apparently, he didn't believe that the color of pasty white skin should be floating around inside an otherwise black blind. Simply wearing dark gloves or covering the windows in shoot-through mesh would have allowed me to arrow that buck. Learning that painful lesson has enabled me to never repeat that mistake again, and to arrow several other great bucks I would never have had a chance at otherwise.

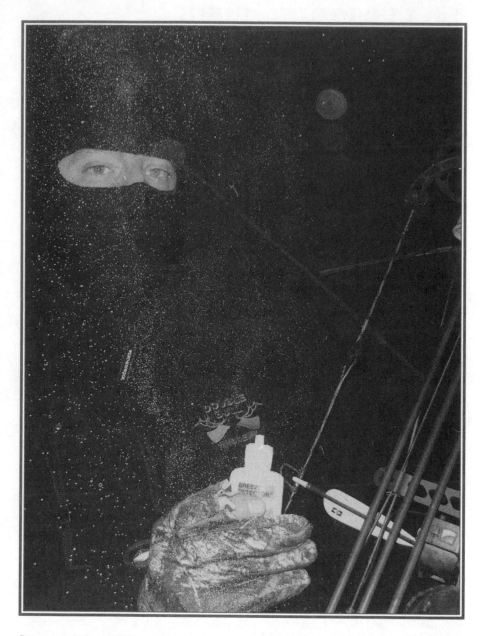

Because of the ability to seal the back side of the blind, air can be forced to flow around it, as opposed to through the blind. This provides scent advantages when deer are downwind.

BENEFITS OF POP-UP BLINDS

As already stated, one of the greatest benefits of pop-ups is their ability to be placed nearly anywhere. Many locations simply don't allow for standard tree-stand hunting methods. Luckily, since the advent of pop-ups, every location is safe to slip a stand into.

A reality of hunting is that many of the largest bucks live in areas not easily hunted. Often, they call the thickest, nastiest tangle their homes. Whether that's a tag-alder or cedar swamp, a young pine plantation, a clearcut regrowth, a pocket of sage or the tangle of thorns that could slice you to shreds, such settings don't often provide suitable trees. The same lack of trees commonly occurs in the more open grasslands of the Western states, where deer can often see danger approaching from what seems like forever away. Pop-ups provide an effective hunting alternative in all of those cases.

They can even be used to help hunters who have issues with getting winded go undetected. Of course, it's always safer for hunters to be downwind of their prey. Still, the beneficial effects of closing windows on the upwind side and sealing the bottom of the blind with debris can reduce the airflow enough to allow them to go unnoticed. This is because sealing the upwind side of the blind causes the airflow to go around, rather than through it. In some situations, that's just the edge needed to tag a mature buck.

SETUP CONSIDERATIONS

When selecting the best location for a blind, one must understand what causes deer to spook at such structures. Aside from not keeping them odor free, I believe the biggest culprit is the element of surprise. I don't believe that deer find blinds particularly threatening. Like a round bale in the middle of a field, it's simply another inanimate object in their world. If given the chance to study it from a distance, they'll often dismiss it as harmless. However, if a deer turns a corner in the woods and finds a new round bale 20 yards away, it's far more likely to turn inside out in an effort to vacate the area. The same is true of blinds.

Considering where deer are most wary helps remove the element of surprise. A prime example is when a deer is approaching an open food source. That same old doe that was calmly walking the trail 200 yards back in the woods is now taking a few steps, stopping and scanning every inch of the landscape before her. If anything is remotely out of place, after a series of stomps and head bobs, she will likely vacate in a hurry, alerting anyone who cares to listen with her barrage of snorts. This tendency makes hiding a blind along the edge openings a challenge.

Conversely, while traveling the transition zone between feeding and

Trimming the lower branches and snugging a pop-up blind under limbs of ever-greens is a great technique for breaking the roof outline.

bedding, deer are far more relaxed. In such areas, hiding a blind is more easily accomplished. First, try to find some hanging branches that you can slip the blind under, located 15-20 yards on the downwind side of the travel zone. Being set off the deer's natural line of sight helps.

Just like with tree stands, being in the shadows also helps. However, keeping the sun out of the hunter's eyes is even more important. During both early morning and late afternoon, because of being on ground level, having the blind's openings oriented toward the sun commonly causes the hunter to look directly into it. Obviously, that can seriously impact the ability to shoot.

A further complication is that having the sun shining directly into the blind creates other serious problems. One of the advantages of quality blinds is that their dark interior helps to hide the hunter. If sun shines directly into the blind, the hunter becomes highlighted and items such as the bow, arrows, hunting heads and other objects are likely to produce reflections.

Keeping the blind in the shadows is one solution to hiding both it and the hunter inside. At the very least, the blind must be positioned so that the sun is off its back side during the hunt.

The next great culprit when it comes to revealing blinds is not brushing them in well enough. If it's in a relatively open location where deer can see it from a distance, doing nothing but popping it up and placing it next to any available cover will work. However, when blinds are placed in thicker cover and deer have a high probability of not seeing them until they are 50 yards or less away, they must be brushed in well to break up their outlines for best results.

Draping the top of the blind with a matt of overhanging branches goes a long way toward blurring the outline. If a suitable tree doesn't exist, snug it into the best available cover and either cut branches for the top or use a concealment product, such as the synthetic branches made by PMI. Breaking the roofline is critical for placing blinds in cover.

Along with using cut limbs or synthetic branches, a great way to break the roof outline is to remove enough of the lower branches from an evergreen to be able to slip the blind underneath (always check to see that it's legal to cut branches and/or get the landowner's permission before doing so). By snugging it under a natural mat of limbs and allowing them to hang over the side, the blind blends in very well. Placing a smattering of natural or synthetic limbs around the outside, paying particular attention to the corners, further aids the blending process.

Remove all the debris from the inside of the blind's floor and use it to seal the bottom around the outside. Doing so helps further blend it in, along with reducing airflow and allowing more silent movement inside. The combination of placing the blind out of the deer's line of sight, breaking the roof and effectively blending its sides dramatically reduces the element of surprise and promotes relaxed shooting opportunities.

Another method of removing surprise is placing the blind in relatively open areas. When deer can see the blind from 50 or more yards away, they have the opportunity to survey it for potential danger. As in the comparison made earlier, the first time they see a round bale in a field, they most often analyze it for a period of time and then dismiss it as harmless. Though a certain percentage of deer will spook from this placement method, I've personally used it successfully several times to fool mature bucks.

HIDING THE HUNTER

The last steps involve hiding the hunter waiting inside the blind. Unlike being perched 25 feet in a tree, deer can spot unmasked ground-level movement much easier. Luckily, there are ways to counter this. For those shooting fixed-blade and certain expandable heads, using shoot-through mesh is a huge help. The mesh reflects light, which eliminates the unnatural dark holes in the blind and helps hide movement.

Wearing black when hunting from blinds helps the hunter stay swallowed up by the shadows.

Additionally, the windows on the back of the blind must be closed. Doing this eliminates having the hunter's silhouette created by backlighting. Blinds that have viewing ports and silent, easy-opening windows have a tremendous advantage here. Unfortunately, deer don't always realize that they aren't supposed to approach from a certain direction. When they do, the viewing port allows the hunter to see them, whereas the ability to open the windows undetected provides the opportunity for the shot.

The final component of undetected movement is wearing black. The only pop-ups I'd recommend hunting deer from all have interiors that are colored black. It makes staying hidden and moving so much easier to get away with. Wearing black allows the hunter to further blend into the dark interior. Because his face must be lined up with the opening to shoot and his hands are closest to the deer, wearing a black facemask and dark gloves is of particular importance.

The main drawback I've found to hunting from blinds is that it gets darker inside faster than when hunting from stands. Though the deer can still be seen easily, the pins on sights tend to disappear. Those planning to hunt from blinds much should strongly consider using sights with superior light-gathering abilities. Though I've never used them myself, I'd guess that lighted pins, where legal, would also be a good choice. Luckily, simply being aware of this issue and addressing it removes the potential for losing legal shot opportunities due to not being able to see the pins.

THE IMPORTANCE OF PRACTICE

To get the most from the blind, it's a very good idea to practice shooting from it until you are comfortable shooting from a sitting position and slipping arrows through the blind's opening. Though clipping the bottom of the opening is one of the few blunders I've managed to avoid, my good friends, blind-hunting visionaries Keith Beam and Brooks Johnson, have done it more than they'd care to admit during the first few years they hunted from blinds. Unless you practice shooting from them, it can be easy to forget that the arrow must clear the bottom of the blind's opening.

Also, if you're planning on using the shoot-through mesh, highly recommended when deer hunting, use it while practicing. Though I've never had it significantly affect arrow flight when shooting fixed-blade heads, I've found it's always best to test these things before it matters!

SEALING THE DEAL WITH DECOYS

Just following what we've covered thus far will enable readers to use blinds effectively. To really push their effectiveness over the top, consider pairing the blind with a deer decoy.

Decoys are great complements to blind hunting because they draw the deer's attention away from the blind. Though concealing blinds along openings can be challenging, placing a buck decoy 40-50 yards out in front of the blind makes pulling that placement off much easier.

When hunting stands, I like to place a buck decoy facing the stand, approximately 20-25 yards out. That way, when the buck circles it to make eye contact, he typically provides a 10- to 15-yard shot opportunity. With doe decoys, a placement of 15 yards away, in a broadside position, fairly consistently produces 15-yard shots as the buck approaches from behind to mount her.

Though those placement strategies are pretty universally accepted for tree-stand hunting, I believe that they must be tweaked for hunting from ground blinds.

First, I use buck decoys almost exclusively when hunting from blinds. One of the reasons for this is that I want the decoy placed as far away from the blind as I can get it, while still having it produce buck encounters within shooting range.

If the blind is hidden along the edge of a field, I can get away with placing the decoy 40 yards out into the field. Along with putting it out farther than normal, I also alter its position so that it's quartering toward the blind, as opposed to facing it directly. That way, if any deer become curious about what the decoy is staring at, their attentions aren't drawn directly to the blind.

The first advantage to using the decoy as a buck is that, as stated earlier, the investigating buck will most often circle to face a buck decoy. Though the distance varies, this act most often brings the buck another 10 yards closer to the blind, resulting in a 30-yard shot opportunity. Since I'm comfortable with this distance, and I want to keep the buck as far out as practical, I find this placement to be the best balance between the two.

Because deer are already on the alert when approaching fields, they are more likely to notice blinds located along the edges. Because of the high likelihood that they won't notice them until they're too close for comfort, the surprise factor leads to a dramatic increase in negative responses.

Because doe decoys aren't routinely circled, they tend not to draw bucks closer than their position.

When the blind is placed out in the open, such as next to a round bale or a clump of brush, it's often possible to cheat the decoy out another 10 yards farther. If the blind is placed between the woods and the decoy, the bucks will most likely angle past the blind, maintaining eye contact with the decoy the entire way. That placement also typically results in 30-yard and closer shot opportunities. If shots 20 yards and closer are the goal, moving the decoy 10 yards closer in on either of these setups will most often accomplish that.

Though I haven't come right out and said it yet, I'm guessing that most readers have already figured out why I want to keep the deer away from a field-edge blind setup. The closer they get, the more likely they are to notice the blind is out of place.

That's more or less the same reasoning behind exclusively using the decoy as a buck. Does tend to congregate around other does. When hunting from a blind, not only are you risking that the does will get nervous because the decoy isn't moving, but there's also the risk that they'll spot the blind. Since does don't investigate bucks very often, going the buck route minimizes the chances that the setup will be swarmed by troublesome does.

Speaking of the lack of movement making deer nervous, there are a few things you can do about that. One is to purchase a remote-controlled, robotic decoy. Legal in most states, it gives you the ability to control head and tail movement, making these decoys much more effective.

Another option, where legal, is to attach a moving tail to a stationary decoy. These are relatively inexpensive devices and, though they aren't as good as the robotic decoys, they do add a level of realism. The completely legal, virtually free option is to tack unscented tissue paper to the ears and tail area of the decoy. By doing that, the tissues flicker in the wind, simulating moving ears and a flickering tail. Any of these options are helpful and can provide wildly exciting blind-hunting moments.

SLIPPING INTO COVER

Of course, though pop-up blinds offer great advantages, owning one isn't a prerequisite to hunting from the ground. For years before their acceptance, countless hunters successfully took deer from the ground without them. Heck, one of the first bucks I ever took with a bow came when I was hiding behind a deadfall.

When selecting a location to hide, use many of the same guidelines as you would for selecting a tree for a stand. You want to be 15-20 yards off the animal's line of sight and have a surplus of back cover. Backing into

Though many hunters may cringe at the idea, sitting on the ground, using nothing but Mother Nature as concealment, can be an effective hunting tactic.

the top of a deadfall, a clump of brush or even using tall grass will work. However, for those concerned with the wind, it's even more critical that this ambush spot be downwind of the deer.

After that, the biggest tricks are to remain motionless and only draw when the buck's looking away. I'm not trying to pretend that hunters won't get busted, but they really can pull this off much easier than most believe. When all else fails, don't be afraid to try it. You just may be pleasantly surprised by the results.

CONCLUSION

Following the guidelines in this chapter will allow readers to get the most from hunting on the ground. Take it from me, not only does adding this tactic greatly expand the number of locations one can effectively hunt, it's just plain a rush to be nose-to-nose with an unsuspecting buck! Try it and see for yourself how addicting that can get. ∎

13. Consistently Scoring on Public Land

When Wisconsin hunter Jeff Severson saw the buck approaching, he couldn't believe his eyes. There, sneaking through a creek bottom, was a buck that would gross score well over 220 inches! More amazingly still, a group of duck hunters was sitting on a pond, pounding away at the skies, merely 100 yards away.

Although he already had an impressive number of Pope & Young bucks to his credit, Jeff knew this one was in a class all its own. Even later, as he walked up to his downed trophy, Severson was amazed.

Certainly, the unbelievable rack was part of the amazement, but where the buck was calling home was every bit as mind-boggling. Despite gaining

Jeff Severson poses with the net 220-inch non-typical monster he took off public land.

exclusive bowhunting access for himself and his small hunting party to thousands of acres of prime Kansas farms, he'd taken this buck from land open to public hunting. Even more amazing, the nearby pond and grass fields were hammered hard by hunters. Yet both the area's sign and reports from nearby farmers all confirmed that the monster buck had called this easily accessed swath of cover home.

As a matter of fact, the only reason Jeff was hunting the area that day was because the duck hunters told him about the deer they saw there. Even with all the sign in the area, Jeff was reluctant to hunt it. With the nearly constant blasts from the shotguns so close to the small patch of cover, he'd decided to give himself only until 8 a.m. before calling it quits.

Frankly, Severson didn't really buy that he was going to encounter a shooter buck there, and who would blame him? After all, what self-respecting mature buck, let alone a world-class monster, would call an easily accessed sliver of cover on public land overrun with duck and pheasant hunters home? Particularly when the buck had endless miles of seemingly better options to choose from. My answer to that is, a very smart buck!

Hunting lands open to public hunting is a vastly different animal than hunting tightly controlled private lands. Often, the same tactics TV and magazine experts preach as deadly are just that, when used on heavily hunted public lands; deadly to your chances of taking a good buck.

Though many hunters fall into the trap of believing that mature bucks don't exist on these public grounds, at least not on the ones they hunt, that belief is incorrect a high percentage of the time. Whitetails are extremely adaptable creatures. It's that very trait that leads many hunters to the incorrect conclusion that the big bucks have either all been killed or relocated off the public ground that they hunt.

The reality is that the bucks able to reach maturity have adapted to avoid hunting pressure, often making them all but invisible during season. Don't believe me? Consider this: In the last three years, I've written 14 stories profiling world-class bucks. When I say world-class, I mean bucks grossing over 190 inches as typicals and over 210 inches in the non-typical category. As I said, world-class bucks. Of the 14, four of them have come from lands open to public hunting. That's just over 28%!

Now, I'd be the first to admit that there are a lot more great trophy-hunting opportunities to be had on private lands than on public. Heck, I sincerely believe that it's easier to take a Pope & Young buck on many of these tightly managed pieces of private ground than it is to take a yearling buck on many pieces of public ground. However, as my non-scientific sampling and personal hunting experiences illustrate, mature bucks certainly do live to old age on pieces of public ground.

The author was able to take this buck by targeting an easily accessed sliver of cover that all the other public-land hunters ignored.

The first trick to taking these mature bucks involves forgetting most of the "cool" hunting tactics you read about and watch on TV. Most of the people teaching them either rely on outfitters to set them up on bucks or hunt such tightly managed ground that they have almost nothing in common with what the average hunter must do to take a good buck. Next, one must avoid hunting like everyone else.

GOING WHERE "THEY" AREN'T

Let's begin this exploration of public-land hunting by addressing that last concern. It only stands to reason that, since a buck successfully eluded the hunting masses to reach maturity, the same tactics that the masses use aren't going to work well on him. Therefore, to be successful, one must break out of the norm.

Doing so begins with the critical first step of hunting where other deer hunters don't. When you pull up to a parking lot overflowing with the trucks of other hunters, it may be hard to believe that there is such a place, but most tracts of public land do have areas that deer hunters rarely step foot on. Finding those pockets is the key.

When scouting public land, the first thing I look for is not pockets of deer; it's the areas that other hunters won't be in. Having hunted public lands every year since I was 12, including tracts in a half-dozen different states and provinces, I've found that these pockets fall into a handful of different groupings.

When most hunters think of getting away from everyone, their minds drift to hiking miles back in to a deer stand. When the area is expansive enough, that certainly is one method. Truth be told, though, even getting one mile from the closest vehicle access point is almost always enough to have the woods to yourself. I have become convinced that hunters must suffer from a rare and highly contagious affliction that causes them to multiply the distance they walk to stands by the minimum of a factor of two. That would explain why so many sincerely believe that they're at least a mile back in, but almost none are over a half-mile from the road.

The next grouping of overlooked pockets runs off the same principle that causes remote areas to go unhunted—the areas that go untouched because they require more physical exertion than most hunters are willing to endure. Three settings that I've hunted immediately come to mind as fitting in this group.

The first was a nice piece of ground in the west-central portion of my home state of Wisconsin. The piece has everything going for it: sizable woods, agricultural land and high deer numbers. Because of that, it comes as no surprise that it's also heavily hunted.

Around a quarter-mile off the crop field, running the length of the property, is a deep gully. Trust me, it truly is a pain to cross, but the rewards were worth it. When I hunted that area, I passed hunters almost every time I was heading to my stands. Yet I never saw a single other hunter on the other side.

Not surprisingly, I did see four Pope & Young qualifying bucks the year I hunted back in there. Frankly, I would have taken pokes at three different bucks in the high 120s, if it hadn't been for the pain that getting them out would have been. Another reason I passed them was the 150-plus-inch

Being willing to cross water barriers can open the door to pockets of virtually unpressured public lands.

10-point that narrowly escaped me. Because he never had a clue I was there, I held out hope that I'd eventually take him. Though I saw him three separate times, two close calls and a distant sighting was all I have to show for it. Still, unless the hunters I spoke to on the field side of the ravine were keeping it a secret, not one of them ever saw any of those bucks there.

I had a very similar experience when hunting in Illinois. There, a square mile of timber was open to hunting. Because one had to sign in and out each day, I can tell you that the place was crawling with other hunters. On the worst day I hunted it, I counted 32 other names. Still, I never saw a single hunter from my stand.

The reason was because three huge ridges ran north-south, paralleling each other. With the only access permitted to the land being from the east and west, despite being less than a half-mile walk in, I knew that I'd have the center ridge to myself. It took two gut-busting, lung-searing climbs to get there, but doing that also resulted in numerous encounters with bucks, including one that can thank an unseen branch for saving his life.

The third location involved a slashing of poplar regrowth, resulting from a quarter-mile-wide strip along the road being clear-cut seven years before I hunted it. Anyone who has ever walked a quarter-mile through a seven-year-old poplar slashing with a tree stand on his back understands that it truly is the definition of hell on earth.

However, the back-side edge, where the slashing met with mature woods, produced several excellent stand sites. For what it's worth, I can tell you that dragging the nearly 300-pound buck I shot from there back through the slashing was harder than walking in with a stand.

The point of these three examples is that most hunters aren't willing to cross major obstacles. Though I had to temporarily agree with their reasoning as I dragged the buck through the slashing, each time I look at him on my wall I remember the rewards of having those types of areas all to myself, despite the hordes of other hunters perched in the easier-accessed sections.

The next grouping of often-untouched pockets also includes an obstacle: water. For some reason, most hunters won't cross water that goes above their rubber boots. Simply slapping on a pair of hip boots or jumping in a canoe has opened the doors for me to many untouched pockets of land on the other side.

Lastly, there's the group that rarely requires extra work to get to—pockets that are often located near the easiest access there is, and are simply overlooked by other hunters. As was the case with Jeff Severson's magnificent buck, sometimes that is due to the established presence of humans. Whether it's because the pocket is close to a house, next to a highway or surrounded by pheasant and duck hunters, bucks learn fast which human activities are a threat and which aren't. Because these human activities drive other hunters away, they also often draw the big bucks in. Spending their daytime hours surrounded by humans in such places, they often live without experiencing a hint of deer-hunting pressure.

Another common type of overlooked area consists of small pockets of trees where there are abundant larger woodlots. That's the perfect description for the area I took another nice public-land buck from. The setting was a large chunk of public land in the central portion of Wisconsin. With big

When on heavily hunted grounds, instead of keying on deer sign, focusing on avoiding other hunters will most often put you where the mature bucks live.

timber and swamps on both sides of the road, everyone ignored the 40-acre native-grass field. About halfway down it, right along the road, stood a small chunk of woods. Because it was impossible to get in and out without clearing any deer inside, it was left alone. However, a quick scout of the area revealed that most deer were bedding in the grass.

Right after climbing into the stand the first time, even before first light, the images streaking through the tall grass were unmistakable. With the deep, telltale grunts following shortly after, there was no denying that the buck dogging the doe was a good one. Over the painfully long 10 minutes it took for shooting light to arrive, they would flash through my field of view numerous times.

Finally, I could make out the buck. Seeing he was a good 10-point, I swiftly decided to take the first ethical shot opportunity he presented. I just needed the doe to lead him back toward the half-acre square of woods my stand sat in.

Before long, she decided to cooperate. From well over 100 yards away, she put on a buttonhook maneuver and made a beeline to my stand. I came to full draw as she approached and I waited until the buck entered the 20-yard mark. With the doe to my left, I voiced a fawn distress call, believing my best chance of stopping the buck lay in stopping his prize.

Mirroring her every move, the buck froze behind her. All that was left was settling the pin behind his front shoulder and willing the arrow to fly true. A series of frantic bounds later, my buck crumpled on the other side of a dirt road. Once again, going where other hunters weren't enabled me to take a good buck out of heavily hunted public grounds.

HUNT CLOSE TO THE BED

The next method of differentiating yourself from the others is, when the tract of land is heavily pressured, forget about hunting the food sources, forget about hunting the funnels, forget about hunting the impressive sign. Mature bucks conduct almost all of the activities those stands are set to take advantage of after dark.

Instead, find his bedding area and, just like during the lull phase, hunt as close as you can get without him knowing you're there. Remember, these bucks aren't like the ones you commonly read about or see on TV. They survive heavy hunting pressure by not making themselves easy targets. Along with avoiding areas with deer hunters when possible, that also means they don't move much when deer hunters are in the woods.

I've recently been seeing a lot of press from an outdoor writer who sings the praises of hunting public land during mid-day. He believes that bucks move then because other hunters aren't in the woods.

Public lands can offer great hunting opportunities, assuming you don't hunt like everyone else.

Though I do admire his hunting abilities and he honestly is one of only a handful of "experts" who hunt in a way I respect, I still must disagree with him. I do fully agree that hunting mid-day is productive on both lightly and heavily pressured public lands. However, on the heavily pressured lands, unless you are lucky enough to have a relatively large pocket to yourself, it has always been my experience that the mature bucks rarely venture far from their bedding areas at mid-day, morning or evening. During legal shooting light, they're close to their beds or they're already dead. So you must also be close to their beds to arrow them.

There are two notable exceptions to this that I've found. One is during bad weather. I believe that some of these bucks have been trained to realize that bad weather drives hunters from the woods. Because of this, they tend to move more freely during periods of heavy winds or rain. That makes those good conditions for hunters to be in the woods.

Don't get me wrong. I personally believe it is unethical to shoot a buck during heavy rains. I've had bucks run close to 200 yards on double-lung hits. During a heavy rain, even finding them would be difficult. If the shot is off at all, with all the blood washed away, it is like trying to find a needle in a haystack. However, the second the rain starts letting up, I want to already be in position!

The other exception is hunting doe-bedding areas during the rut. Even heavily hunted public-land bucks sometimes fall prey to having the desire to breed overpowering their better judgment. Not only will they abandon the safety of their bedding areas to stay with a hot doe, they'll also get up and follow her if she insists on moving. That makes setting up on her bedroom a good option.

Both hunting his bedding area and hers was already covered in Chapter 5. However, one intense method of hunting his wasn't. When he absolutely, positively refuses to move during daylight, it's time to go in after him.

This strategy hinges on beating him into his bedding area. That may require being in stand as much as two or three hours before first light. Even if you beat him in, chances are high that it will still be dark when he returns to his bed. That means you'll now have to remain undetected until shooting light arrives. If he's bedded within shooting range and in the proper orientation, the shot can be taken then. If not, it demands waiting until he eventually stands to relieve himself. This is a demanding and risky tactic that should be saved as a last resort, but it can work when he is only willing to move after dark.

DON'T DRAW ATTENTION

Keeping with the theme of hunting differently from others, heavily hunted land is not the place for calls, decoys or rattling. These bucks survive by avoiding anything out of the ordinary. Since this survivor has resisted coming to every other hunter's calling and rattling efforts, don't be arrogant enough to believe he won't be able to resist yours.

Along the lines of keeping a low profile, this is also not the place to trim large shooting lanes. Just because these warriors avoid hunters during the day doesn't mean they aren't being educated by them during the night. You can bet that he's investigated the disturbances created by freshly hung stands many times before. I can't tell you how many times I've tracked deer in the snow that purposefully make wide arcs around other hunter's stands. Believe me, they know what's up when the ground is suddenly littered with cut branches and a three-foot-wide lane magically appears.

As on more lightly hunted lands, I strive to do any significant clearing of lanes in the spring. Even then, I do far less pruning on heavily hunted public lands. Besides, it isn't legal to prune anything on many public lands. When placing stands during season, I never nip more than a branch or two, even when legal. When I'm forced to do that, I use a pruning tool to avoid leaving fresh sawdust behind, and I remove the branches from the area. The last thing I want is to raise a buck's curiosity and have him come in to investigate the area after dark.

Between following my odor-reduction techniques, limiting pruning to a minimum and not leaving curiosity-raising sawdust behind, I lower the odds of having to pass the sniff test.

TOOLS OF THE TRADE

Several products and tools can make hunting public lands easier. The first are a mountain bike, bike light, rack and bike lock. With a rack on back to strap your bow to and a light to show the way, a mountain bike can let you get way back in much easier than walking on many of the larger tracts of public land.

However, when you're either hunting way back in or on the other side of difficult obstacles to cross, you must remember that, assuming you're lucky enough to arrow Mr. Big, you also have to get him out. That's where a good deer cart can come in very handy. They may not work well in seven-year-old poplar slashings, but they can save many sore muscles in a lot of other settings. As a side note, when there's snow on the ground, the kid's long plastic snow sled works even better.

Lastly, though it should be a given that the hunter already has studied a topo map to help him find the unhunted pockets, he should also bring that map out hunting with him. Along with a flashlight and compass or GPS, topo maps are very helpful if you get turned around. For any of you who have tracked many deer after dark, you fully understand how easy that can be. The difference between doing so in farm country and on a large tract of public land is a slight inconvenience verses a long night in the woods.

CONCLUSION

When you really think about it, there are two categories of mature bucks that most of us will encounter over our hunting lives. There are those that are exposed to heavy hunting pressure and those that endure moderate pressure. The tactics you read about in many articles and watch on a lot of TV shows will work, to various extents, on the properties experiencing moderate pressure, such as many family farms or your typical lease.

Truth be told, a lot of these hunting methods are ideally suited for hunting the third category of mature bucks: bucks that receive extremely light and tightly controlled hunting pressure. For the minority of hunters who are lucky enough to chase these bucks, almost everything they try is more effective. Unfortunately, most of us will never experience that kind of hunting.

When deciding on hunting strategies, the first step is determining which group the bucks you're hunting fall into. Then you can truly analyze which strategies make sense. Taking this critical step gives hunters a fighting chance on any piece of whitetail ground.

Luckily, despite what many hunters believe, mature bucks do exist on many tracts of public land. Just remember that they are true survivors and our hunting tactics must be tailored to that fact. Find the pockets where other hunters aren't; set up near the buck's or does' bedding areas, depending on the phase of season; take advantage of the times other hunters aren't in the woods; and, above all else, don't draw attention to yourself. Do those things and you just may be surprised at how many mature bucks your area's public lands hold.

Last, but certainly not least, don't forget your map and compass! If you spend much time in the big woods, you'll thank me for that piece of advice later. ■

Studying topo maps will help you find the pockets not touched by other hunters. Having a compass will help you get back out again!

14. Understanding and Taking Advantage of Weather

It was late December, the temps had dropped well below zero, and a biting wind was ripping at my cheeks. Luckily, my attempts at dressing to beat the cold had worked and I was loving life. A full three hours before dark, I already had seven deer within 50 yards and was supremely confident that the weather conditions would cause that number to steadily grow.

My confidence was justified. As the next two hours zipped by, a steady stream of deer piled down the ridge on the opposite side of the narrow cornfield. As the stream began to turn into a trickle, he appeared.

As the large-bodied nine-point entered the field, a mere glance caused a young buck to scurry away. From the reaction of the other deer, it was obvious that he was the dominant buck in the area.

Understanding how deer relate to weather was a major factor in taking this large buck.

Truth be told, it was the antics of two immature bucks that provided me with the break I needed. Specifically, I can thank a 2.5-year-old eight-point for harassing a little fork horn. After playfully sparring, he got too aggressive for the little guy and chased him near my stand. Securing the release to my loop, I positioned my feet for what I hoped would happen next.

The big guy, with his attention focused on the pair from the start, puffed up and began stomping his way over. Hoping the scrappy eight would stand fast, I raised my bow and readied for the shot. At 20 yards, Mr. Big altered his head on approach to my stand and turned to make eye contact with his subordinate.

Coming to full draw, I settled the pin behind his front shoulder. In an instant, the buck exploded into the air, kicking violently before bursting across the field. Slanting farther to the side with each yard he covered, he horseshoed his body as he crumpled to the ground.

A topic that is seldom given the consideration it's due is how weather affects whitetails. Sure, most hunters understand that high temps can shut down deer movement. However, that knowledge is most often used by hunters as ammunition to convince them to sacrifice a hunt, as opposed to figuring out how they can adjust their strategy to best accommodate the weather's effects. Frankly, those who attempt to compensate for the weather have a significant advantage over those who don't.

BARKING AT THE MOON

Unfortunately, many more hunters plan hunting trips and strategies around moon phases than around the weather. I say unfortunately because I believe the idea that the moon has anything to do with timing the breeding phase is a load of shingles. Sure, it sounds cool and most definitely provides a topic that sells articles and books, but I don't buy into it for a second.

Don't take my word for it. That's every bit as risky as taking what the moon "experts" say at face value. Instead, listen to the true experts on whitetail biology. Retired deer biologist John J. Ozoga and Warnell School of Forestry's Dr. Karl V. Miller are two of the most highly respected whitetail researchers in the nation. These gentlemen have studied deer and conducted research at levels that no outdoor writer could ever pretend to attain. Knowing them personally, I can tell you that they are about the only true experts from whom I accept what they say regarding whitetails almost without question. Not coincidentally, they both are extremely careful not make claims they can't substantiate, offer alternative explanations whenever possible, and aren't afraid to admit when they are unsure.

They graciously agreed to allow me to say that they don't buy the idea of the moon phase or position having anything to do with timing the breeding phase either. In the northern Michigan square-mile enclosure where Ozoga conducted years of research, John pointed out that the peak-breeding phase occurred every year within a matter of a few days of the established baseline, regardless of the date of the full moon. It is important to note that this is not simply his opinion. This is stated in the mountains of data he collected on wild deer held in captivity.

In the northern regions of the whitetail's range, proper timing of fawn drop can be of critical importance to fawn-survival rates. When does are bred early, there is a high risk of the fawns being dropped into a relatively cold, snow-covered world. Being born into these conditions decreases their odds of survival, and so does the winter-stressed condition of their mothers. Because a doe is still fighting for her own survival, she is not in a physical state and does not have the required nutrition available for the same level of milk production she can achieve after spring green-up occurs.

On the flip side, when northern fawns are born late, they face an unnecessarily increased challenge to survive, having less time to mature before the fall's shortening photoperiod triggers the body to stop growing and shift its resources to fat production. Though a late-born fawn still commonly has an impressive layer of fat, its body is smaller than a fawn dropped at the appropriate time, all else being equal. The smaller body size not only prevents them from reaching as high for winter browse, but it requires more energy to heat one body-unit. Then, there's also the increased difficultly of traveling through deep snows.

Though there are more disadvantages to fawns being dropped early and late, it should be clear that a significant shift of breeding dates according to the full moon would be counterproductive to the northern whitetails' survival rates. As brutally cruel as Mother Nature can be, she doesn't play needless games like that.

Based in Georgia, Dr. Karl V. Miller provided me with an interesting southern slant. In a nutshell, he pointed out that the peak breeding dates vary by weeks, some places even months, as you travel across many of the southern states. Jumping from state to state, the peaks vary wildly, all the way from September to January. Since each state and regions within the same state share the same moon, it's hard to believe that the moon phase dictates when peak breeding will occur. Instead, it's much easier to believe that these variations are due to regional differences in habitat, weather patterns and even the importation of deer to the region.

The ultimate kicker for me is that if breeding dates were based on the moon, it would be easy to scientifically prove it beyond any doubt. Unlike the challenges of trying to determine what messages are conveyed by the

In all regions of the whitetail's range that experience prolonged harsh winter conditions, the proper timing of spring fawn-drop is far too important a survival factor to leave breeding up to the moon to dictate.

odors left at scrapes or the significance of each gland on deer, proving the moon's control over breeding wouldn't be riddled with myriad factors or be widely open to interpretation.

No, if the moon controls breeding to the extent that some writers claim, all one would have to do is document fawn-drop dates or examine the fetuses of road-killed does for a couple of years. Either way, factoring in the standard gestation period would swiftly prove the moon's value.

I apologize for jumping up on my soapbox for so long and preaching on this issue. It's just that I feel a tremendous loyalty to those who buy my books, read my articles or come to see me speak. It wasn't that long ago that I had a nine-to-five job. I clearly remember the challenges of saving vacation time for hunting and striving to ensure that I selected the best possible times to be in the woods. I also clearly remember how ripped off I'd feel when I bought a book or read an article that was trying to sell me on a hunting technique or product that I doubted even the author believed in. If you get nothing else from this book, at least don't waste your valuable saved vacation time by investing it on hunting according to the moon's ability to control breeding dates. If you do, I firmly believe that you're basing your trip on a fallacy.

THE MOON'S EFFECT ON MOVEMENT

With all that said, it may surprise some to find that I do believe the moon's phase and positioning likely has an impact on whitetail movements. However, before I continue, I must point out that this, like everything else in this chapter, is based exclusively on my experiences, the hunting logs of the outfitters I work with, and educated guesses. There are so many potential factors that can affect why a wild deer chooses when to move that I believe nailing down absolutes is nearly impossible.

At the very least, the moon can be a source of light. I say can be, because heavy cloud cover can block the light of even the brightest full moon. The difference between going for a walk on a cloudless, full-moon evening verses the same night with heavy cloud cover, or a night when a sliver of the moon is in the sky, is significant. Because of that, I strongly suspect that it also impacts whitetails.

As stated earlier, a major problem with determining how moonrise and phase impact deer is trying to account for all the variables. For one, I have no doubt that more movement will occur during all portions of daylight on a property that receives little pressure than on a heavily hunted tract of public ground. Then, regardless of the moon phase, northern deer will undoubtedly move less on a November day with temps in the 80s than they would if the temps were in the 20s. All in all, I believe weather conditions, hunting pressure, the phase of season and even food availability all have a more significant impact on deer movement than the moon's phase or position.

With that in mind, and all else being equal, I do believe that the following guidelines are sound: The first is that I've experienced the best morning and evening movement when the moon is between a quarter and three-fourths full. When a three-quarter or greater moon rises before or within several hours after sunset, my logs show that my afternoon hunts are typically less productive than my morning hunts, and mid-day endeavors tend to be a little better.

Close study of my logs clearly shows that the phases of season, food availability and weather conditions all play a more significant role in getting deer on their feet or keeping them bedded down. However, if I'm trying to plan a five-day hunting trip to Wisconsin, I'd earmark a period between October 28 and November 7 that would give me five full days of the moon falling between a quarter and three-fourths full. After that, I'd hope like heck for a day with moderate winds and temps in the 20s and low 30s.

WEATHER THAT GETS BUCKS ON THEIR FEET

If there are weather conditions that hamper deer movement, it stands to reason that some conditions are conducive to increased movement. Ultimately, how a weather condition contributes to safety or comfort is the determining factor in whether or not it's a primer, a hindrance or non-factor as applied to deer movement.

Before we begin covering the weather factors that encourage movement and, later, the ones that discourage it, keep in mind that I'm comparing them to days when all other factors are equal. Just because the weather conditions are ideal doesn't guarantee that the deer you're chasing will be moving more. As I've already said several times, a host of factors can affect that. Conversely, as you'll find out, just because the weather is bad for movement doesn't mean you should stay home.

Since everyone seems to get pumped for hunting cold days, let's start there. Because of the superior insulation deer's coats provide, up until late season, temps that range from 5 to 15 degrees below normal definitely appear to encourage more movement. You can understand why by asking if you'd rather wear a parka and climb ridges on a 50-degree day or a 35-degree day. Obviously, the comfort factor plays a large role in this.

During the post-rut phase, temps in that range and even further below normal may actually stifle overall deer movement, but benefit the hunter. When it's nasty cold out and breeding is over, deer must ultimately concern themselves with surviving winter. The line between life and death is often based on how much energy a whitetail can conserve during this portion of season and all the way up to spring green-up. So they will spend more energy-conserving hours in bed on colder days to save body heat.

Since the nighttime and early-morning hours are commonly the coldest in a 24-hour period, and being up and feeding at such times would result in the burning of increased calories, from an energy-conservation standpoint, deer are more likely to select the less-draining option of feeding during the comparatively warmer late-afternoon and early-evening hours. So during the late season, a general rule of thumb is that the colder it gets, the better stands on the food source can be.

Next, falling or rising barometric pressure tends to get deer on their feet. Because storms can shut down deer activity, the tip-off of falling barometric pressure encourages them to go feed one last time before bad weather hits. Rising pressure, on the other hand, lets them know that the storm has passed and it's safe to feed again.

Overcast skies, light fog and light rain, sleet or snow all also encourage deer movement. In each case, the conditions reduce visibility, but not so much as to seriously hamper whitetails' vision. My guess is that these conditions enable deer to remain hidden more easily without making them feel blind. In the case of light precipitation, it also allows deer to move more quietly. Along with that, moderately moist air enhances the white-tail's sense of smell. Finally, those conditions can reduce the amount of overheating that deer wearing a thick winter coat experience in mild temps.

Lastly, light winds allow whitetails to take better advantage of their eyes, nose and ears. Since they rely on all three for survival, one can assume that deer feel safest when those senses are running at peak efficiency.

Because all the conditions on our list are advantageous to deer, it makes sense that they can inspire increased deer activity.

WEATHER THAT DRIVES DEER TO BED

Based on the weather conditions that encourage deer movement, one could correctly guess many of the ones that slow them down, without even needing to check the hunting logs. As good as temps 5-15 degrees below normal are, temps 10 or more degrees above are bad. Once again, it's the comfort factor.

During late season, extremely cold temps cause deer to move less, shifting much of their movement to the warmer late-afternoon and early-evening hours.

Temps that drop 25 or more degrees below normal slow things way down because of both the comfort and energy conservation factors. However, as covered earlier, that can become an advantage to hunters during the post rut. Really, who cares if overall deer movement is lessened, if it results in increased movement occurring during legal shooting hours? Under these conditions, afternoons are the time to be in the woods. When temps are this low during the late season, you may as well mirror the actions of deer and stay in bed during the morning hours.

Next, it should come as no surprise that heavy precipitation, unnaturally high winds and very dense fog are all movement suppressors. These conditions seriously hamper a whitetail's sense of smell, hearing and/or sight, and since they rely on each for survival, deer have incentive to hole up and wait for better conditions before they move.

Keep in mind that deer have the ability to adapt to almost any given circumstance. For example, high winds to a Kansas plains deer are a tornado to his eastern cousins. If these plains deer had to wait for a 10-mph wind to move, they'd often spend a unacceptably high percentage of time in bed. The same can be said for whitetails living in the large swamps that commonly produce heavy fog. As with many things, these are relative terms and don't apply to every situation

MAKING THE BEST OF BAD SITUATIONS

In a nutshell, effectively hunting conditions not conducive to deer movement requires finding where deer will hole up and hunting close by. During the really cold snaps that occur before late season, in the absence of high winds and heavy cloud cover, look for southern ridge points, knobs and hillsides with a southern exposure. Here, deer can soak up the rays of the sun to help heat their bodies.

If high winds accompany the cold, valleys that block the wind are good choices. If that valley contains a thick stand of evergreens, all the better.

Those thick stands of evergreens can also draw deer well during heavy precipitation or during the extreme cold periods of late season. In both cases, they serve to help protect the deer from the elements.

When it's excessively hot, windy without the cold, or there's dense fog, hunt close to the buck's normal bedding area during most of season and doe-bedding areas during the chase and breeding phases. In the case of extreme heat, established bedding areas are still the place to be, assuming they are shaded. If not, the stands of evergreens can also be good, as can areas that offer shade near watering holes.

Under any of those conditions, don't count on a surplus of deer movement. As I stated at the beginning of this section, when hunting in condi-

Warm temps during late season may be more comfortable to hunt in, but they also drive more of the deer movement to after dark.

tions not conducive to deer movement, one must hunt close to where Mr. Big will be spending the day. Though I try not to repeat myself, that's important enough to say twice.

Another tip for hunting warm temps, be sure to set the alarm and get out there for the morning hunt. Though many hunters believe that high temps delay the breeding phase, research has shown that's not true. However, it certainly does drive it toward the cooler nighttime hours.

With afternoon being the hottest portion of the day, most bucks will hole up then, often not getting up on hot days until sunset or later. The best chance for making something out of nothing during mid-day on through the afternoon hunt is often setting up on watering holes. On the flip side, with morning being the coolest portion of the day during hot conditions, that's often when bucks put in the lion's share of their daylight movement.

If you recall the buck I lured in by the doe-bedding area with scent back in Chapter 10, on hunting the wind, what I left out of that story was that it was toward the end of November and the temps were breaking into the mid- to upper-70s. In the upper Midwest, that's extremely hot for that time of year.

I had hunted two days previous to that morning sit. Both mid-day periods were filled with watching nothing but squirrels. Hunting the afternoons was slow, without a deer sighting until after sunset. But the first two hours of daylight were magical each day. Wasting a morning hunt on unseasonably hot days is wasting the most consistently productive part of the day.

CONCLUSION

When you come right down to it, no matter how many hunting details we can and should address, no hunter has ever mastered controlling the weather or the moon. However, we certainly can control how we approach hunting under adverse conditions. Understanding how they affect deer and how we can alter our tactics to maximize our odds allows us to score during challenging times. The desire and ability to accomplish just that is what separates the good hunters from the great ones. ∎

15. Deadly Scent Tactics

quirting buck lure on the ground as I approached the stand that covered the big scrape, I had no idea how much this day would shape my future hunting tactics. By conserving the lure carefully, I was able to create a scent line nearly 100 yards long.

I don't pretend that I really knew what I was doing back then. I was simply a young kid who wanted to shoot a buck. In my efforts to try something new, I just assumed that this could stir up some action.

I was right. Not long after I climbed into my stand, a young buck came excitedly trotting down the scent line. To this day, I can still remember how the little eight-point's nose was glued to the ground as he hurried along the dribbles of scent.

I can also remember how he stopped cold upon reaching my tree. Not knowing any better, I had dribbled the scent line no more than two or three feet away from my stand, onto the scrape. Looking back, the buck must have picked up the odors from where my sweaty hands gripped the 2x4 I'd nailed into the tree as a step.

Apparently, there must have been deer scent mixed with my own human odors. The buck's head would cautiously draw near the step, only to snap back as he retreated a bound. Then the allure of scent would draw him cautiously forward, only to send him leaping back again.

As this was going on, imagine being a young boy, sitting on a branch about 15 feet up in the tree. Though I'd been lucky enough to take a couple of deer already, they were more by accident than skill. Heck, just seeing a deer from stand was an event. I'd certainly never had a buck come so close as to sniff my tree before. Even if the buck had positioned himself perfectly and there were no branches in the way, I doubt if I could have shot him anyway.

Some time after the young buck beat his eventual retreat, I was finally able to pull myself back together. Just about the time I did, the sounds of another rapidly approaching deer tied my stomach back into knots.

This time, there was a little fork horn working its way along the scent. In his excitement, he blew right past the stand. Hitting the scrape, he was investigating it in earnest as I sent the first arrow over his back. After a startled jump, he searched the area for the source of the phantom noise. During his search, I accidentally hit him in a lethal area with my second shot.

I say accidentally because I took out a major artery in his rump. That was something I omitted during the many times I told my friends the story of my great hunt. I always made a big deal of watching him bite the dirt after going only 50 yards. The location where I hit the buck isn't important and should be completely forgotten. What should be noted is that I was hooked on using scents from that day forward.

As some people who have followed my work closely have read before, I was using scent when I took darn-near every good buck I've ever shot. The day I took the large nine pictured in the last chapter, I was using doe urine as a cover scent, as was the case with both the 10- and nine-pointers from the Hunting the Wind chapter; the 150-inch buck, also discussed in that chapter, was lured in with Special Golden Estrus. That same scent hung near where both of the bucks in the chapter on hunting public land were arrowed, as well as the wide eight that fell in Chapter 8. The 3.5-year-old nine-point in Chapter 9 had his nose glued to Active Scrape when the arrow hit. Then there's the 160s buck that begins Chapter 4. He was following a scent trail of Special Golden Estrus to the mock scrape he'd worked earlier, which held the same scent and also had a Scent Dripper filled with Mega Tarsal Plus hanging over it. I could continue, but I think you get the point.

What seemingly flies in the face of all that is my firm belief that most hunters have unrealistic expectations of what scent can and will consistently do for them. I never bank on a scent drawing deer to me. Sure, there are times that I set out a scent strategy with the hope that it will happen. But what I actually consistently expect scent to do for me is stop a deer in my shooting lane and—unlike using a grunt to stop him there—focus his attention on something other than me. That gives me all the time I need to calmly place the pin and make a relaxed shot.

STOPPING BUCKS IN THEIR TRACKS

The benefit of using scent to stop a buck for the shot provides serious advantages over grunting at him. The first is that I've never sent a buck running scared from scent, although I have spooked deer by grunting. Let's face it, they realize that a grunt isn't supposed to come from 25 feet up a tree 15 yards away from where they're walking. Hunters can get away with the grunt to stop bucks more often than not, but a certain percentage are going to choose the flight option instead.

Even when the grunt does stop them, now they're hunting you. Their senses are on full alert. That makes the risk of them jumping the string much higher. It also means that after looking and not finding the buck 15 yards away, either up the tree or on the ground, they're likely to get nervous and may leave in a hurry. That can make the times they don't stop at the right angle or in an opening a real problem.

When using scent to stop bucks, it must be placed upwind of where

The possibility of stopping a buck in a shooting lane can be enhanced by using scent to draw his attention away from the hunter.

the buck will pass. Obviously, if it's downwind, he'll never smell it. Next, remember that the scent should be positioned so that the deer stops at both a comfortable shooting distance and in an opening capable of slipping an arrow through. Then, all that's left is to place a scent wick at about a buck's nose level and juice it with your favorite scent.

When bucks investigate a scent wick, they stop and focus all their attentions on that odor. That provides the hunter ample time to take aim and squeeze off a relaxed shot.

REELING THEM IN

When it comes to reeling bucks into shooting range, the biggest trick is to have bucks already searching for the scent you're offering. For example, on Halloween, an estrous trail on the downwind side of a doe-bedding area will likely produce more consistent results than one running across an alfalfa field. Chances are good that the buck cruising the doe-bedding area already has his mind set on locating an early doe. When he hits the estrous scent, it is simply giving him what he's after. He's far more likely to be focused on safety and feeding as he enters the alfalfa field. Not coincidentally, he's also more likely to ignore the estrous scent there.

During the second rut, the odds of that same buck responding to an estrous scent placed in a picked cornfield are much higher than the alfalfa field example. Certainly, feeding may be on his mind, but he realizes this is his place to score the few remaining breeding opportunities of the year. As a side note, when that estrous odor accompanies a doe decoy, he's likely to come in on a run. The point is that using scents when and where they make sense is a huge part of drawing bucks.

When approaching the stand from downwind of a scrape or the downwind side of a doe-bedding area, I'll lace a rag tied to a string with estrous scent, freshening it with a few more squirts every 10-20 yards until I reach the stand. Unlike when I created the scent line in my youth, I now know to make a loop at about 15 yards around the stand location. Doing this provides several excellent shot angles. Upon drawing even with the stand, I stop applying scent. From there, I proceed to the scrape or bedding area. Lifting the drag, I return to the stand and hang it where I want the shot to occur.

Now, when a buck is scent-checking the scrape and/or bedding area, he believes he has found what he is looking for and is likely to follow the trail. Because of the extra squirts the rag received, the trail gets stronger as it approaches the stand. That helps ensure he follows it in the right direction. Because of the arc made around the stand, he should provide ample shot opportunities.

As opposed to catering to a buck's desire to breed, mock scrapes can be used to threaten a buck. They work particularly well when placed in the same vicinity as a primary scrape that is well suited for hunting (see Chapter 5 for how to select productive scrapes to hunt).

When scent is placed higher than a buck's nose can reach, it can draw him to the general area, but often doesn't freeze him in a specific location. That can be advantageous when trying to draw bucks in closer yet with a second scent wick, but is most often a disadvantage when that's not the case.

HOW TO CREATE A MOCK SCRAPE

Prepare a licking branch by selecting a limb the approximate diameter of a pencil. If a licking branch isn't already about five feet from the ground, one can be bent down from above or attached to the tree.

Clear obstructing debris from the forest floor in the immediate area around the scrape.

With the tip of the licking branch pointing downward to the top edge of the scrape, create an oval of bare dirt approximately three feet wide and four feet long.

Hang some form of lure dispenser above the scrape. I prefer Scent Drippers because they only dispense the scent during daylight hours and last over a week. This both encourages deer to visit during daylight hours and minimizes the number of trips I must make to the scrape to keep it charged.

Fill the dispenser with dominant-buck urine, squirt a little estrous urine in the scrape, and walk away.

The message this sends another mature buck is simple. "The breeding phase is approaching fast and a new buck is threatening to steal your does. You better kick his tail and show him who's boss before it's too late." By adding estrous scent to the mix, it adds a further sense of urgency. "Uh oh, a hot doe's already in the area. Regardless of whether you're going after him or her, you better act fast!"

Aside from mock scrapes and scent trails, I'll also use scent when decoying. Depending upon which sex I choose for my decoy, I place some doe or buck urine on the ground between its back legs. Because I don't want my decoy to get rancid and want to keep the ability of switching it between being a buck or doe, I never place scent directly on it. With the proper scent, you will be appealing to the buck's sense of both sight and smell. Toss in some grunts or doe calls and you've got hearing covered as well. The more senses you address, the more convincing your lie becomes to Mr. Big.

COVERING MY TRACKS

Another way I rely heavily on scent is to cover my tracks. I do this by applying non-estrous doe urine or non-rutting buck urine to boot pads. That way, each step I take, I'm depositing some non-threatening urine.

When I get into the stand, I remove the pads and hang them from branches within reach of my seat. Though you'll soon find out exactly what I think of cover scent, I do believe the odor of urine helps set other deer at ease.

In reality, I only use a handful of different scents: doe and buck urine as cover scent; estrous-doe urine on scent wicks, sprayed on scrapes and when creating scent trails; and rutting-buck urine with tarsal glands or a mixture of hot-doe, young-buck and fawn urines in scent drippers over mock scrapes and on scent wicks. Still, based on all the scent questions I receive, I feel I should explain each group of scents and lures.

COVER SCENTS

Cover scents may be the most misleading group on the market today. Many companies try to sell the hunter on the illusion that the cover scent will stop deer from smelling them, regardless of how much human odor the hunter is emitting. In my early days, I used to buy into that myself. I routinely doused myself with skunk essence before a hunt. Not only did that hurt my popularity, the deer that passed downwind would turn inside out as they bolted away. Even worse, many would stop after a ways and snort for what seemed like forever. The problem is that deer can smell multiple odors at once, regardless of how pungent one of them may be. Draining the bladder of non-estrous does and young bucks is a way of capturing cover scent.

ATTRACTANTS

The next group is attractant and curiosity lures, intended for use mostly during early and late season. Most often, they are a food-based scent or emit a non-threatening fragrance that's geared toward appealing to a deer's curiosity. For do-it-yourselfers, vanilla, anise oil and beaver castor will each work and are the basis for many curiosity scents.

TERRITORIAL INTRUSION

Territorial intrusion scents are nothing more than dominant-buck urine with or without tarsal glands added. They are used to make the local big guy mad and want to fight the newcomer. A great source of this scent tarsal glands from mature, rutting bucks. They can then be cut off and used immediately or frozen for use next season. When cutting them off, be sure to wear rubber gloves. It's also a very good idea to double-bag them in zip-locks before tossing them in the family freezer. They really stink. Also, be warned that using truly dominant-buck urine and tarsal glands will scare some subordinate bucks away.

SEX SCENTS

Finally, quality sex scents consist of pure estrous-doe urine and vaginal secretions. Though you can drain an arrowed estrous doe's bladder, my first

Using estrous and territorial-intrusion scents together on mock scrapes appeals to a buck's desires to both breed and defend his turf.

question would be why you'd want to shoot the best buck bait available? Save that for before or after the breeding phase. Next, several studies I've read indicate that the urine itself is no more attracting than the urine of non-estrous does. The attracting qualities appear to be picked up as the urine is passed out of the doe.

CONCLUSION

Provided that you don't buy into the hype, scents and lures can provide the hunter with pleasing results. The key is to use the right scent at the right time. When bucks already have their minds set on finding what you're selling, scents bring far better results.

However, one must also be careful when using these products. When investigating an odor, a buck's sense of smell is obviously working over-time. That means if you're sloppy about leaving your own human scent behind, you're likely to receive a negative result. Make sure you don't touch scent wicks or scent drippers with bare hands. Also, don't breath on anything. That may initially sound silly, but breath odors clinging to objects around the scent can also generate negative responses.

Speaking of negative responses, remove the scent wicks when you leave the woods. If not, you risk lowering the effectiveness of your attrac-tant. For example, let's say you're using a food or curiosity scent. A half-hour after you leave, Mr. Big trots by downwind. Smelling this appealing odor, he comes in to investigate. If you're lucky, all he finds is a scent wick.

When bucks investigate a scent, they expect to find something. With estrous scents, he expects to find a scent trail or a doe. A mock scrape is also an answer to why a sex or territorial intrusion scent is there. With food or curiosity lures, they expect to find food or something of interest.

When he checks out your food or curiosity scent after you've left, the first risk is that he'll smell you. Even if that doesn't occur, he found nothing that rewarded or satisfied his interest. Now, two days later, you are hunting a stand in the same area. When he smells the same scent again, will he come in to investigate? Last time he wasted his efforts. Leaving the scent in the woods effectively lowered the odds of receiving a positive response to that scent on future hunts. The more times he investigates it after you've left, the lower those odds become. Use scents intelligently and they'll be much more effective. ■

16. Making the Shot

I could feel my heart sinking in my chest. As the bear tried to navigate the clutter of the woods, it would travel five yards and lie down, go another five yards and lie down again, get up and lie right back down. After seeing the bear fall flat on its face twice, I actually felt sick that I hadn't ended its misery, and vowed that if he came back I would take the first ethical shot provided.

When the 200-plus pound spring bruin had come in, he'd been walking down an obstacle-free cut line. It was obvious by the way he contracted his front leg and relied on the other three to walk that he had been injured. However, it appeared that he had adapted nicely and it wasn't causing him serious issues. With my first tag filled with a Pope & Young bear, I had my heart set on filling the second with either a good-sized color-phased or 400-plus pounder. Because of that, along with the bear not appearing seriously hampered by his injury, I'd convinced myself that passing the shot was justifiable.

Now, sitting in the pop-up blind with my cameraman, Trevor Wilson, I felt like the biggest heel to walk the face of the earth. The only question left was, in the 80 minutes of shooting light remaining, would I have a chance to redeem myself?

About 30 minutes later, Trevor spotted the bear out approximately 60 yards from the bait. He was working his way through the tangle of timber to get another helping of meat. To clearly illustrate how badly injured this animal was, it took over 45 minutes for him to cover the 60 yards to the bait, never traveling more than five yards before laying down and actually falling several more times.

Finally, after what seemed like an agonizing lifetime, he was at the edge of the woods, preparing to make the last few yards to the bait that sat 12 yards from the blind. Sitting there in a head-on posture, he scanned the area for several minutes, simultaneously trying to muster energy and be completely certain that he was safe.

Numerous times, his gaze hit our blind. Each time he looked right through it, never having a clue that anything was out of place. Obviously, we'd done an acceptable job of concealing the newly set pop-up to completely dupe a mature bear that'd been made ultra leery from fighting and its severe handicap. Any doubt I could ever have about the effectiveness of a properly blended pop-up was washed away forever.

The ability to consistently make shots, like the one made on this wounded bear, is only one of the advantages of catering practice technique for real-world hunting scenarios.

Coming to full draw as the bear finally got to a standing position, I waited for it to make its last few labored steps. Approaching the bait in hurried labored lurches, it snatched a scrap of meat and began spinning to leave. It was now or never. Quickly guiding my pin to behind the front shoulder, I took advantage of the split-second opportunity and sent the arrow into flight during the bear's turn.

The crashing noises that followed him through the timber ended shortly, followed immediately by the death moan a successfully placed arrow can bring. I'd been given a second chance and succeeded at doing the right thing.

I know this is a book on deer hunting, but I decided to begin this chapter with the story of that hunt because it does a good job illustrating why one should cater practice techniques for hunting. The first reason is that if I'd either wounded that majestic warrior further or not been given a second chance, even if I'd eventually tagged a 500-pound stud of a blonde bear, I'd have regretted that hunt for the rest of my life. It may sound sappy, but it's the God's honest truth. Deep down, I needed to make that split-second, whirling shot as much for my own sake as the bear's, and my practice techniques allowed me to do it.

Before you take that last statement as being arrogant or boastful, I don't pretend to be a good shot. I'm being completely sincere when I say that I don't deserve the credit for the high-pressure, seemingly difficult shots I make. In my being able to pierce both lungs on a twirling bear, while simultaneously feeling the weight of the world on my shoulders, the practice techniques I use deserve 100% of the credit.

I have no doubt that if I practiced like most hunters, I would not have made that shot, or many others that I've made. Heck, I wouldn't be surprised if 50% or more of those who read this book would beat me at tournament shooting.

However, when an animal steps within my range and provides a shot, it's already dead in my mind. That's because I don't practice nailing the 10-ring on targets. I practice killing animals. That, my friends, is a completely different approach to practice, and it makes the shot at the moment of truth an unconscious, mechanical act. Under those conditions, assuming you put in the practice time, you almost can't help but make the shot.

WHY TRADITIONAL PRACTICE FALLS SHORT

Before we plunge into taking practice to the next level, let's look at a traditional practice session. Grabbing the bow as you walk out the back door, you head for the 20-yard marker for a target. With feet planted squarely on the ground, you focus on your form and take your time to place the pin perfectly as you toss three or four arrows at the target.

After you gather your arrows, you move back to the 30-yard mark and repeat the process. You may even go crazy and then shift back to 40 and fling some more. Arrow after arrow, you shoot from predefined markings, while dressed in a T-shirt and jeans, in the totally controlled environment of your backyard. It's even most likely a calm and sunny afternoon. Having grouped well, you head in the house, feeling good about how well you've shot today.

Now, let's look at a real-world hunting situation. From behind the tree stand, the hunter hears the snapping twigs and crunching leaves of deer coming in fast. Turning to look, he spots a shooter buck dogging a doe. As she streaks behind the stand, the hunter comes to full draw. Grunting with his mouth, the buck stops. Unfortunately, several branches and twigs separate our hunter from his prize.

In the fading light of the closing minutes of hunting hours, the stand sways gently as the hunter struggles to hold on target. Guestimating the distance to be 30 yards, our hero determines that the arrow should slip through. With his body contorted to its fullest extent possible, he places the 30-yard pin the best he can and lets the arrow fly. At the same moment, the buck decides to leave in a hurry. As the arrow snips a tuft of back hair, our hero's heart sinks.

Our hero was I, shooting at one of the first good bucks I'd accidentally bumped into during my youth. Looking back on it, my form was wrong, the buck was actually 18 yards from my stand, it was pure luck that the arrow didn't hit a branch, and I'd never practiced during windy conditions or in fading light. Frankly, aside from sighting-in, I'd done next to nothing to prepare myself for making the shot.

PRACTICING THE KILL

To practice shooting deer, one must radically deviate from traditional practice techniques. After shooting enough from predetermined distances to get sighted-in, the only reasons to continue this type of shooting are to build shooting muscles, assure that the pins are still on, prepare for an archery shoot, or just because circumstances don't allow for other forms of practice. To practice killing deer, one must address some major factors that aren't accounted for during traditional backyard practice sessions.

First, there is the difference in form. Though it can occasionally happen, rarely does one shoot at deer while in a normal standing position with both feet on the ground. Next, one must be able to range the animal fairly accurately, and shooters have a significant advantage if they possess the ability to determine whether their arrow can slip through holes in the vegetation. Of course, not succumbing to buck fever is also a critical component, as well as having archery gear and clothing that do not sabotage the shot.

Setting tree stands in the backyard for practice allows hunters to work on their form until maintaining proper form, while contorting the body in every likely shooting position, becomes a reflex.

As you can see, these factors are rarely if ever addressed during normal practice sessions; it's no wonder so many shots are blown. It's almost like trying to hit a home run in professional baseball game without having had spring training or batting practice. Luckily, we can tailor practice techniques to address each of these factors, and more.

ADDRESSING REAL-WORLD SHOOTING FORM

Beginning with shooting form, how many shots at deer have you ever taken that didn't involve sitting or bending, as well as contorting the body to some extent? If done without adjusting one's form, these actions can significantly throw off shots. Heck, it's hard to even remember not to just drop the bow arm down when shooting from a stand, let alone to hold your form, if you've never practiced bending at the waist.

When considering real-world hunting form, think of it in the terms that an archery pro once used to help teach me: "When using proper form, you should be able to draw a straight line from your bow hand, through your release and out to the elbow of your release arm. As long as you keep that line straight and parallel to your chest, you can twist your body in any way and the shot will fly true. Bend that line or put it at an angle to your chest, and it throws a monkey wrench into the engine."

To make maintaining proper form second nature, practice from the positions you find yourself hunting in. If you hunt from a tree stand or pop-up, practice from it. Also, divide your practice shots between sitting, standing and kneeling. Chances are, regardless of the position you prefer to shoot from, you will eventually be caught in situations that demand shots from each of these positions.

To illustrate how to practice maintaining proper shooting form, let's look closer at practicing from a tree stand. When shooting at an object from a tree, the first step in maintaining proper form is bending at the waist to avoid dropping the bow arm down to the target. Bending at the waist allows the shooting line to stay straight and parallel to the chest.

To get in the habit of maintaining proper form, you must practice from a tree stand. Until it becomes second nature, start each practice session by picturing an imaginary target that's straight above the real one, at a height that is vertically in line with your position. Draw the bow and aim it at the imaginary target. Then, bend exclusively at the waist until pin rests on the real target. That is proper shooting form when the hunter is positioned higher than the target. When the target and hunter's positions are reversed, you must bend back at the waist to rise up.

To incorporate contorting the body into practicing proper form, purposefully set your feet at a 90-degree offset from the target. Imagine the target at your vertical level and in the horizontal position that your feet are set for. After drawing and aiming at the imaginary target, bend exclusively at the waist to get to the ground and then twist only your hips until the pin is on the real target. Practicing various angles and every awkward position that could occur will make maintaining proper form in real-world hunting situations become second nature.

NAILING YARDAGE

With the availability of quality range finders, a lot of hunters seem to believe that the ability to judge yardage isn't as important as it once was. I tend to disagree. For one thing, there haven't been many bucks cooperative enough to stand in one place long enough for me to dig out the range finder, get a reading, put the range finder away, come to full draw and shoot.

Sure, one can and should use a range finder to mark trees; that can certainly help. But the uncooperative nature of bucks seems to dictate that they show up where we don't expect. That translates to them not always standing next to trees we have marked.

Along with that, a major goal of practicing to kill is eliminating the need to think. The need to think and remember is what prevents shooting from becoming an automatic reflex. When the reflex has been trained properly, it enables the hunter to know the animal is dead before shooting, as well as making it reality a high percentage of the time. Relying on memorizing the yardage to a bunch of trees around the stand almost begs hunters to allow excitement to cause them to forget or make a mistake.

Finally, there are many situations when the hunter isn't going to be able to perform these marking rituals: A great buck shows up at first light on a stand's first hunt; while walking in, you spy one laying in the tall grass; or the buck appears in an open field. For all these reasons and more, being able to accurately judge yardage at a glance is still very important.

The first step in making yardage estimation more accurate involves incorporating it into practice. To do this, purposefully shoot from random locations, estimating the distance before letting the arrow fly. Then pace the distance off when you retrieve the arrow.

Routinely estimate distances in everyday life. For example, while walking through a store, in the woods, a parking lot, or any other conceivable location, pick an object you're approaching and estimate the distance. Count your steps to get there and you have the answer.

When sitting on stand during dull times, pick objects and estimate their yardage. Then pull out the range finder and correct yourself. This is

Range finders are great tools for honing yardage-estimation skills while killing slow periods on stand.

not only a great practice technique, but it also serves to mark trees.

A word of caution is in order. When shooting from a stand or in steep terrain, remember that the horizontal distance is what matters. At a sharp angle, a deer can be 35 yards away from you, but if the horizontal distance is only 25 yards, shooting it for 35 will cause the arrow to go high. To further complicate this, distance tends to become distorted when viewed at a sharp angle.

To help counteract extreme angles, I've found it easier to use objects that are horizontal to my position to estimate yardage. For example, if the buck is standing next to a straight tree, one can estimate the tree's distance at eye level and use that to determine what pin to use. Together, all of these practices make yardage-estimation skills more of a reflex, and more accurate.

SLIPPING ARROWS THROUGH THE EYE OF A NEEDLE

Understanding arrow trajectory is also important. Most every hunter realizes that an arrow's path follows a slight curve, yet many have difficulties determining whether they can make it through small openings. Those who use sights can easily remove much of the guesswork.

When confronted with a small opening, the first task is estimating its distance. To make it simple, let's say that a buck is standing 30 yards away, with a mat of twigs forming a softball-sized opening at 20 yards. If the 20-yard pin falls in the opening when the 30-yard pin is placed on the buck's vitals, the shot can be made. If not, you're going to send the arrow into the mat of twigs. This scenario works with any distance, so long as you accurately judge the distance to the animal and the obstructions.

Knowing this is helpful, but practicing it is even more beneficial. As opposed to setting a target in the wide open, place it so that you are forced to shoot through obstacles. The more that is done, the easier it becomes to gauge whether or not the shot can be made. Surprisingly, understanding arrow trajectory enables you to take many shots that look impossible, and stops you from taking many that look good but are doomed to end tragically.

BEATING BUCK FEVER AND EQUIPMENT ISSUES BY MAKING IT REAL

Beating buck fever is something we can control. Most experts claim that the true trigger for both buck fever and target panic is the fear of failure. I do not know if that is the case or not. However, I know that

I personally suffer less from shooting stress and nerves if I've repeatedly practiced the scenario I'm facing.

To that end, I strive to make practice as real as possible. I place a deer target in the woods, slap up a stand, get dressed in hunting clothing and pretend I'm killing the target. I even go so far as to pretend the deer is walking through the woods, pick my spot to draw, wait for it to enter the opening and shoot. While doing this, I follow the imaginary path of the buck the entire way and play it out as if it were really happening. After the shot, I even pretend to watch it running away and note the landmarks it passes.

The more real the act becomes, the less nerves I face when truly taking a shot at a buck. If I feel that I'm succumbing to nerves, I tell myself that this shot is no different from the countless others I've already taken at targets. Because I consistently pulled them off, I can do this just as easily.

A final advantage that making practice real provides is the ability to test hunting equipment and clothing. Before I use any product or clothing of significance in the woods, I practice with it. If a sleeve is going to catch the string, a head is going to alter my arrow's impact point, a flap on a facemask blocks my vision, extra layers require adjustment in form, or a glove torques the release, I want to know before the moment of truth. All of these steps remove many of the rogue factors that can rear their ugly heads and ruin otherwise perfect shots.

CONCLUSION

Several other issues should be addressed before closing out this important chapter. The first is to use practice to learn your limitations. Practicing while bending and twisting, in wind, rain, fading light and any other condition likely to be encountered, provides the chance to learn about your own and your equipment's capabilities and limitations. Let's face it, if you can't consistently make a 40-yard shot in high winds when it doesn't count, your odds of making it when it does count are even less. Learning limitations and accepting them is a vital component in ensuring a successful shot.

There's another advantage to pushing some limitations in practice beyond what you feel confident with in the woods. For example, I always practice at least 20 yards farther out than I'm willing to shoot at a deer. Flinging numerous arrows from 70 and 80 yards sure makes a 30-yard shot at a buck seem like a chip shot.

Finally, practicing various angled shots on deer targets and learning a

Placing deer targets in the woods, wearing hunting clothing, and shooting from stands when you practice addresses many of the issues encountered during shots at real deer.

deer's anatomy can open the doors to more ethical shots than just broad-side and quartering away. For years we've been taught not to take any shot that deviates from those two body orientations. Though I'd never recommend taking any other that wasn't practiced often, so long as the arrow can be slammed solidly into the vitals, the shot is possible. Since each hunter has different capabilities, I cannot tell you what shots you can ethically take. To find out for yourself, thoroughly learn whitetail anatomy and experiment with deer targets.

Always err on the side of caution. We owe it to the animals. If that's not enough alone, though I strongly recommend taking the first good, ethical shot opportunity offered, you never know when passing a marginal shot will lead to a chip shot. ■

As opposed to shooting in the backyard at known distances, placing a target in the woods and shooting from random locations is better practice for the real hunt-ing-world shooting skills required.

17. Blood-Trailing Techniques That Produce

Hearing the unmistakable sounds of a swiftly approaching chase, I immediately positioned myself for the shot. Spotting the doe coming in on a run, the mature 10-point hot on her tail, I came to full draw and hoped I'd catch a break.

As they blew through my shooting lanes, I didn't even attempt voice grunting him to a stop. Though it's arguable that I may have been able to stop the monster buck, the odds of it being in a position that offered an open shot were pitifully low. On the flip side, attempting that act would all but guarantee that the doe wouldn't return. Instead, I did nothing and played the odds of her eventually leading him back around.

Seconds after the pair vanished over the edge of the ridge point, I heard another deer coming in fast. Twisting around for the shot, I spotted the nice eight-point. Though he barely qualified as a shooter, I had only one day to hunt and decided, if given the opportunity, that I'd take a shot. Since he was taking up the rear by himself, I also knew my odds of stopping him were greatly improved.

Coming to full draw as he neared my shooting lane, I noted his location relative to the double-trunked maple and prepared to voice grunt at him. A split second before the eeeerrrrrrp was about to leave my mouth, he stopped on his own. Placing his nose to the ground, he sniffed the bed of a doe that had moved on an hour before. Placing the pin, the arrow traveled the 28 yards separating us and sliced high through the buck's chest cavity.

In an explosion of flight, he tore away. As I followed his path, I noted the fallen tree he leapt, the clump of brush he avoided and, finally, the large oak he swung around. Shifting over to use my ears as eyes, I listened closely, trying to continue following his path as he crashed away out of sight.

With the last sounds gone, I immediately returned my attentions to the precise location the shot occurred, marking the spot just ahead of the double-trunked maple with a neon sign in my mind. Next, I focused on replaying the shot, noting the exact position the buck was standing, as well as the point of impact of the arrow. Visualizing the angle, I estimated the path the arrow took through the buck's chest. If I was correct, the head sliced the top portion of the closest lung and blew somewhere out about 25% down the far lung. It should have caught both lungs, but definitely higher than I preferred.

With that surmised, I painstakingly re-created the buck's every bound. I remarked the fallen tree, clump of brush and large oak. Now, all that was left was to kill the rest of the 30 minutes before climbing down by replaying the events until I couldn't possibly forget my mental markers.

Finally, the time arrived to climb down. Gathering my gear as quietly as possible, I slowly slipped over to the location of the shot. Stopping a couple yards shy of the location, I glanced at the double-trunked maple, then over my shoulder at the stand and back to my mental marker to verify my position. Assured I was in place, I began systematically scouring the forest floor before me, scanning with my eyes from left to right, up a foot and then back over to the left. After scanning back and forth five times, visually covering the first five feet, I stepped forward and repeated the scans.

Spotting a tuft of hair, some blood splatter and then the arrow, I stepped forward again and investigated each in earnest for clues. The presence of long brown hairs and absence of white didn't rule out a high lung hit. The tiny speckles of bright red blood neither confirmed nor denied it. But the bright-red arrow, with a smattering of pink, foamy blood, did validate that lungs were involved to some extent.

Not being confident that I'd caught both lungs, I decided to back out and get my friend Mike Strandlund. Having set him in a stand some distance away from mine, I slowly covered the third of a mile to the truck, shed some clothing and took a leisurely stroll to get him. After discussing the morning's events, we both returned to the truck. Mike dropped some of his nonessential gear and we returned to the scene of the crime, almost two full hours after the shot had occurred.

With the location of impact marked, my mental markers of the buck's path and a good flow of blood, the trail began easily. However, it kept going. After following it for approximately 200 yards, I began to get a little nervous. My bow had been nocked with an arrow from the start and I was prepared for a follow-up shot the entire trail. With Mike following the flow of blood, I had treated this more as a stalk than a blood trail, increasing the odds of being able to unleash an arrow swiftly.

After following the trail 100 yards without recovering an animal, I always once again contemplate whether backing out and giving it more time is the proper course of action. In this case, the deer had already been given extra time, the blood trail was strong, it had yet to bed down and we hadn't heard any sounds of a deer crashing away in front of us. To be honest, I would have backed out and given the situation even more time if any of that had been different.

Somewhere around 250 yards away, we saw him. Lying in a ditch, the eight-point had toppled over as he walked. Closer examination showed that

Despite this buck traveling over 200 yards after the shot, following the proper trailing techniques made his recovery easy.

it was indeed a high double-lung hit. With only one day to hunt, I'd managed to both shoot and successfully retrieve a fine eight-point. I was supremely pleased!

THE CRITICAL MOMENTS BEFORE YOU START TRACKING

I began this chapter with the story of this eight-point's demise because it illustrates so many of the trailing techniques I was taught and learned as I grew as a bowhunter. Sadly, it has become obvious to me through numerous conversations with hunters that properly trailing deer is becoming a lost art. A surprising number of hunters no longer understand the basics.

The first is to mark the precise location of the animal when the shot occurs. Though many things are running through a hunter's mind the moment before unleashing the arrow, one of them had better be picking a marker that enables him to find the location again. If that isn't done, a lot of extra, potentially sign-destroying tromping of the area can occur.

Next, follow the flight of the arrow and note its exact impact. Your ability to accurately do this and note the whitetail's exact position is the foundation of the entire tracking job. If the foundation is shaky, you may still recover the animal, but the odds of that happening are decreased.

With those two steps out of the way, focus on the whitetail's escape path. When doing so, strive to note the landmarks it passes. Right now, everything seems to be happening at warp speed. Picking landmarks along the deer's path is the only way I can consistently slow the event down enough to be able to retrace its path in my mind later.

After the deer vanishes from sight, see with your ears. Doing this requires listening to both the direction of the sound, to maintain the animal's path, and for clues on what it's doing. Obviously, splashing sounds indicate it hit water, a prolonged crashing of brush suggests it's bolting through a thicket, if crunching leaves is all you hear, it is likely in the mature section of woods and, finally, rolling or kicking noises suggest that the deer is down. Analyze what you hear and do your best to make sense of the sounds.

Once the woods go silent, immediately replay all the events in your mind. The time for congratulating yourself is when you've found the deer and not a moment before. Use the time between the shot and beginning the retrieval process to analyze the events and formulate a game plan.

Rewinding to the shot, look at where the deer was standing and mark it again in your mind. Next, see the arrow's impact, its angle and the angle of the deer. Did the arrow pass through or was it still lodged in the deer? If it's still in the deer, how deep was the penetration? Did it take out the lungs or heart? Was it a gut shot, a liver shot or maybe strictly muscle? Answering these questions accurately is the key to determining a tracking strategy.

Some will certainly disagree with me on this, but the only times I immediately take up the trail are when I see my deer drop or it begins to rain or snow. Otherwise, I always try to give the deer at least a half-hour to die. Frankly, once those situations have been removed, the only time I even consider taking up the trail after 30 minutes is when I'm supremely confident of a double-lung or heart shot.

If there is any doubt, or the arrow or hair indicate otherwise, I'll give it at least two hours. Under those circumstances, when the shot occurs in the afternoon, I'll wait until morning. A good Coleman lantern is the best tracking light I've found, but it's no substitute for tracking a deer when a second arrow may be required. When I believe that's a possibility, and rain or snow isn't likely, I always wait until morning.

If the shot occurred in the morning, the more iffy the shot, the longer I give it. The generally accepted rule of thumb on a gut shot is four hours, but when there's enough light in the day remaining, I prefer six on any hit farther back than the rib cage.

FOLLOWING THE TRAIL

Regardless of the hit, the first step is inspecting the shot location. Whether I'll check it on my way out or after returning with help depends on whether I believe I can get to the site and out without spooking the potentially wounded deer. If I'm safe, I want to get answers as soon as my 30 minutes in the stand are up. If not, I'll err on the side of caution.

When inspecting the shot location, look carefully for blood, hair and the arrow, assuming a pass-through. I'm not a whitetail-hair expert, but three different hair traits are obvious clues. White hair is rarely a good sign. Think about where white hair is found: under the chin, along the bottom of the belly, the tail area and inside of the back legs. Unless an odd angle was involved, the presence of white hair almost always screams "back out now." Another bad sign is the presence of the short hairs found on the lower portions of the deer's legs. Brown, normal-length hair is what I hope to find.

As far as blood is concerned, medium-red or frothy pink are my first choices. Frothy pink obviously indicates a lung shot. Medium-red simply says it isn't a gut shot. Gut shots often provide a watery blood. Of course, finding chunks of food or a stink on the arrow also screams gut shot. Finding the arrow is helpful because it typically provides both blood and hair to examine.

Once I've determined it's time to go after the animal, I want a partner. As we'll cover later, if the trail is lost, the more the better. However, until that point, I've found that more than one helper is too high a risk, due to the increased movement possibly disrupting sign and the increased noise generated by extra people.

When involving a second hunter on a blood trail, be sure to carefully explain what's happened and what you expect of him.

The reason I want that second person is so that I can focus on stalking the deer. Before I begin the trailing, I explain that I want them to be the bloodhound. He must go slow, not jumping ahead until blood is found, and be very quiet. My goal is to find the deer dead. If it isn't dead, I intend on stalking to within bow range and shooting it again.

That's where giving the deer extra time provides a side benefit. It's a given that the extra time allows the deer to die. But it also gives the deer an opportunity to lie down, and as it's lying down, it's getting stiff. Within reason, the longer it lays, the stiffer it becomes and the less it wants to get up. Several deer I've shot a second time saw and/or heard me coming. Still, the extra time had worked to stiffen them to the point that I was able to slip within bow range and get a second shot anyway.

In fairness, I should point out that the longer the deer lies, the more likely it is that clotting will occur and blood loss will slow or stop altogether. That's the foundation of the argument to push deer as hard and fast as possible to keep them bleeding, and increases the odds of them bleeding out. I'm not arguing with the validity of that; I've just found that the approach I use is a viable alternative. It works best for me.

To take full advantage of my approach, you want to be scanning ahead the entire time you're on the trail, ready for a rushed shot. That requires someone else to follow the trail. While they're slowly following blood, I'm flanking them a couple feet to the side in predator mode. If the animal is spotted, I signal my partner to stop and move in on my own.

My approach can also be used when a hunter is forced to trail a deer alone, albeit not as easily. Beginning at the point of the hit, scan down the path the deer took and try to pick it out in its bed. Pay particular attention to anything that provides superior cover, such as a clump of brush, the tops and roots of fallen trees, tall grass, or anything that can potentially hide the animal.

Once the careful and thorough scan of the area is complete, resume following the trail for some distance. How much cover the area provides dictates the distance to go before you stop to scan again. If tracking through a relatively open area with little cover to hide in, you can go farther than when tracking in a thicket. Use common sense, and err on the side of caution. I doubt there is a single reader who will follow a blood trail too slowly.

Along with looking for blood, keep an eye peeled for other clues. Bent grasses, snapped saplings, upturned leaves and clods of fresh dirt can be significant. When all else fails, put your face close to ground level and look for signs left from where the deer was running or walking.

Though sometimes you must venture ahead of the blood to find the next spot, try to keep that to a minimum. Each time you jump ahead, you risk destroying sign and make noticing the deer's disturbance to the ground more difficult. When you must do so, be sure to check the ground for sign before each step.

Also, while on a difficult trail, be sure to use a marker of some sort. Toilet paper works well because it's biodegradable. Flagging tape also works, but make sure to take it out with you. Either way, markings allow you to keep track of the last sign found and show the deer's flight direction.

WHEN BLOOD IS LOST

The troubling thing to me is what happens when some hunters lose blood. Unfortunately, way too high a percentage of ethical hunters turn around and go home. I say ethical, because they really do care and feel bad. They simply don't know what else to do. I'm confident that most of the people reading this section know how to track deer. Some of you most likely are better than I and are reading this hoping to simply pick up a trick or two, which is a strong indicator of your abilities to become even better still.

However, an alarming percentage of the newer hunters really have no idea how to trail a deer. Many of them aren't kids, either. I still remember clearly when, back before I became a full-time outdoor writer, a coworker in his mid-40s told me about a deer his hunting partner shot. Both he and his friend had been rifle hunting since they were kids and had picked up bowhunting in the last few years.

To make a long story short, his friend shot a buck, they followed it about 100 yards, and then the trail ran dry. After looking right around the area where they lost blood for a while, they left. My coworker felt horrible and didn't quit out of laziness. The two of them simply didn't know what else to do.

Though each situation is different, I do have some general guidelines for when blood is lost. If the deer is following a trail, I continue following it while maintaining the stalk/blood-trail technique, all the while scanning for blood and the deer.

If that turns up empty, or if the deer wasn't following a trail to begin with, try to imagine where a wounded deer is most likely to head. That is commonly water or tick-protective cover. If either exists in the path of travel, stalk/blood trail your way to that destination.

Another guideline is the saying that badly wounded animals don't head uphill. Though I have found more than a few exceptions to that, if there isn't a strong reason for them to go there, they are more likely to head downhill. Never rule out the uphill search, but checking the lowland first is typically a better choice.

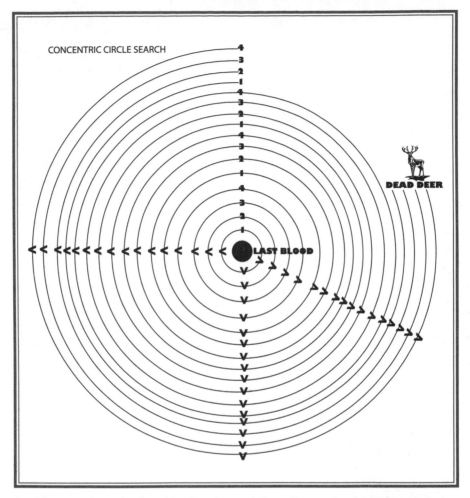

In this example, we've lost blood and rounded up three other hunters to help us. Each member of the group of four is spaced 50 yards from his closest search partner. With helper four marking each circular path, the group members stay spaced 50 yards apart while conducting their sweep. If one of the group loses visual contact with the partners on either side, the entire group tightens to thoroughly check the thicket. In this case, the buck was found on the fourth pass.

OK, so you've checked the trail and obvious locations. The deer is still unfound. Now is when a group comes in handy. Return to the location where the last blood was found and begin a systematic, concentric-circle check of the area.

When doing this in a group, fan the party out in a line going away from where blood was found, spacing them no more than 50 yards apart. Make that spacing less if there will be areas where visual contact times between the closest party members on either side of you cannot be maintained at all.

As the circle around the blood is made, all members are looking for both the deer and signs of blood. Also, the person on the outer ring should mark his path.

When the circle has been completed, shift everyone out. Now, the one closest to the blood must remain in visual contact with the markings from the last circle. Continue repeating this process until all the habitat has been covered, or the deer or fresh blood is found. If fresh blood is found, return to the stalk/blood-trail method until blood is either lost again or you realize a successful outcome.

Obviously, doing this alone takes more time, but it can be done as effectively. To pull it off, mark each circle you make. When one circle is complete, shift out no more than 50 yards from the marked circle and swing around again, marking as you go. Repeat the process until the deer has been found.

NEVER SAY DIE

Of course, some deer are only superficially wounded and continue to live long lives. In those cases, one must eventually give up the search. However, far too many hunters give up on blood trails too easily, and both they and the animals pay the price.

That's where persistence becomes the tracker's best friend. When it comes to retrieving deer, never underestimate the power of having a never-say-die attitude to turn an otherwise horrible waste into a tremendous feeling of satisfaction.

A buck that two of my guide friends were involved with illustrates this perfectly. The hunt really began when Alberta's Northern Wilderness Outfitters' guide Shawn Rempel spotted the magnificent buck while driving the back roads, looking for deer. From that point forward, Shawn and outfitter Larry Jolliffe made it their mission to have one of their clients take the double-beamed, drop-tined monster.

Over a month later, Eastern hunter Tom Nitterour was lucky enough to get the first crack at the stand that would produce the only shot at the buck. Just as the sun rose, he began to realize just how lucky he really was.

After what seemed like watching the buck for a lifetime as it walked the 300 yards to Tom's stand, the moment of truth finally arrived. When the buck entered easy shooting distance, it detected that something wasn't quite right. As he turned to leave, there was a tree blocking Nitterour's shot. At 40 yards, the buck presented a slight quartering-away shot opportunity. Tom let the arrow fly.

"He tore off back toward the crop field," said Nitterour. "The whole ways I'm begging him to drop. Finally, he stopped at the other side.

This great buck traveled somewhere over 800 yards after the shot, the retrieval of him clearly illustrates the value of a never-say-die trailing attitude.

I thought I could see my arrow in him, so I figured he'd go lay down and die. I got the shot off, I knew I hit him and I kept telling myself that's all I can do for now. I played the waiting game."

Finally, the time came for Shawn Rempel and Tom Nitterour to begin looking for blood. After unsuccessfully scouring the field, they decided to get help. In actuality, it was outfitter Larry Jollife who finally found blood—over 800 yards away from where the buck had been hit! When their tracking eventually resulted in kicking up the buck, they decided to come back the next morning.

Almost a full day after the initial shot, having pulled out to regroup and go after it again three times, Tom Nitterour finally stood over his buck of a lifetime. When everything else fails, having a never-say-die attitude can make all the difference in the world. When properly applied and paired with addressing the seemingly little details, that attitude can have a huge positive effect on nearly every aspect of bowhunting trophy bucks.

CONCLUSION

Following the guidelines set forth in this chapter can be a big help in retrieving deer. As with most everything in life, the hunter's skills at blood-trailing deer will improve with practice. The more often you follow a blood trail, the easier it gets.

That's where many hunters fail to take advantage of the opportunities they have. As my brother Joe reminded me to include in this chapter, just because you see a deer drop doesn't mean you shouldn't follow its trail anyway. Almost every time Joe or I watch the deer fall, we eventually trail it from the shot location to where it crumpled. Why? Because every time a blood trail is followed, it provides an opportunity to learn.

As far as learning is concerned, tracking deer that the hunter has been able to watch drop can be a better learning tool than those that must be tracked. In this case, the hunter has likely witnessed everything the deer did during its final dash. What sign is left when a deer jumps a log, how does the trail differ when the animal is running versus walking, and how does the sign reveal that the deer came to a momentary stop? All these questions and countless more can potentially be answered and applied to other trails, because the hunter saw for himself what the deer did. All that's left is to match the sign to the acts that occurred.

Another reason this can be a superior learning tool is that the pressure is off and the hunter can focus exclusively on sharpening his tracking skills. That can also be done by retracing the path of a successful blood trail, but concentrating more on what each piece of sign tells you, instead of allowing eagerness to pressure you into immediately trying to find the next drop of blood.

Heck, you could even try to convince your friends to allow you to follow the blood trails of the deer they take. If they are willing to let you do that, but unwilling to participate, all you need to know is where the shot occurred and go from there.

Finally, returning a day later and following the trail is also a good idea. Day-old trails look radically different than fresh blood trails. Such an exercise makes finding the deer left overnight in the woods an easier and more familiar task.

I have no doubt that some readers are scoffing at these ideas. All I ask is, before you brush them off as ridiculous, think of how much time you spend practicing with your bow. Isn't the ability to follow a blood trail every bit as important a skill as being a good shot? If it is, when given the opportunity, doesn't it make sense to practice this skill? I believe the answer to both those questions is a resounding yes! ∎

18. Remembering Why We Hunt

It was by far the most fun I've ever had hunting. As the sun rose to kiss the dew-drenched meadow, my daughter Elizabeth and I sat quietly in the turkey blind. As I pulled out various calls, Beth, only 6 years old at the time, would giggle up a storm at the sounds they produced.

After kindly reminding her she needed to be quiet several times, I remembered why we were here. We were sharing the blind that morning to have fun bowhunting turkeys. When I realized that, I handed her a box call and asked if she wanted to give it a try. I can still clearly remember her looking at me sheepishly as she asked if I was sure it was OK.

Some of my most memorable hunts involved either shooting does or nothing at all.

Ultimately, bowhunting is about building memories and sharing good times with family and friends.

Upon assuring her that it was fine and that she didn't need to worry about doing it wrong, she proceeded to make some of the most unnatural and horrible sounds a turkey call has ever produced. With her laughing hysterically after each one, it wasn't long before she had me clutching my side and tears of laughter running down my own cheeks.

Not surprisingly, we didn't see a single turkey that day. That didn't dampen her enthusiasm in the least. She enjoyed herself so much that morning that she came with me each day of Wisconsin's brief turkey season.

Rising well before first light, we'd share a hearty breakfast, get our gear together and head for the blind. Each morning, as the sun rose, bone-chilling turkey calls and hysterical giggles filled the otherwise serene setting. I can't begin to imagine what any other turkey hunter hearing us might have thought, and frankly I don't care. I was hunting the land I used to own and sharing a hunt with my daughter that I'll cherish for a lifetime.

No, we never did see a turkey that season. However, to this day, mere mention of that hunt lights up my daughter's face like a sign above a Las Vegas casino.

When it comes right down to it, that is why we should bowhunt.

Ultimately, shooting trophy bucks should merely be a nice byproduct of achieving our goals. When you scrape away all the hype and hoopla, the true mission should be to have fun and build memories to be cherished.

Don't worry, I'm not going to jump up on a soapbox and go on and on about this for pages on end. However, I do feel this chapter is necessary.

I fear that we as bowhunters are starting to lose focus on what our sport is all about. We have shifted to worshiping the mighty antler. Because of that, we lock down our hunting lands and don't even allow our friends and neighbors to step foot on our sacred ground. Chances are good that we'd get more furious at the idea of someone trespassing than if they'd stolen our wallets. Soon, nothing hunting related becomes more important than killing that massive buck. In fact, doing so has become so critical to us that we scorn and ridicule those who dare shoot a fork horn.

Don't get me wrong, I love chasing the big boys and don't believe there is a single thing wrong with that. I also realize that my description, thankfully, doesn't fit everyone.

My only point is, please don't get so fixated on antlers that you forget to have fun. The majority of the most enjoyable hunts I've ever had revolved around sharing them with my children, shooting a doe, matching wits with a monster buck or simply experiencing something in the deer woods that I've never seen before.

That, my friends, is what I believe bowhunting should be about. When you think about it that way, the pressure to take Mr. Big is removed and the impressive set of antlers you end the season with is simply a bonus— a reminder of why we were out there to begin with. We are there to build memories and enjoy the splendor of the deer woods. ■

APPENDIX

RUT DATES TABLE

Early season: Approximately the first two weeks of season; shorter in areas of intense pressure and longer if hunting pressure is minimal.

October lull: Begins when buck sightings dry up on the food sources and continues until right around October 25.

Peak Scraping Phase: Begins about October 25 and runs until the mature bucks begin seriously chasing does.

The Chase Phase: On or about November 5, the woods explodes with bucks chasing does. This phase lasts approximately five days.

The Breeding Phase: November 10 is commonly the day that serious breeding activities really ramp up. Some breeding occurs before this phase and some after. Still, until around Thanksgiving Day, bucks will be primarily focused on breeding.

Late Season: Begins as breeding activities wind down and runs until season's close.

The Second Rut: I personally don't believe that a date can be set on this phase. It happens when it happens. Still, most, but not all, second-rut breeding activities I've witnessed have occurred in the last three-and-a-half weeks of December.

These dates are not to be applied everywhere. They are specific to the central portion of Wisconsin. The farther south you travel, the more the peak scraping, chase and breeding phases are drawn out and overlap. In the Deep South, the date of the onslaught of the breeding phase ranges wildly.

This table is merely meant to approximate when these phases occur for much of the whitetail's range. For those hunting in the North, Northwest, Midwest and Northeast, the table can be adjusted to fit pretty well. To do so, simply change the beginning date of the breeding phase for what matches your area—a call to the local big-game biologist can provide that date—and push the dates for the other phases up or back by the same number of days. Though it won't account for phases being stretched as one travels south, it will get you pretty close.